CW01494788

WHITESHILL CHURCH

The life and times of an early nineteenth-century village chapel at Hambrook in South Gloucestershire

Researched and written by Howard Berry

Copyright © Howard Berry 2017

i

Acknowledgements

Thank you to those long-time church members who have helped me put this account together through providing information, memories and photos from days gone by at Whiteshill - and answered my endless questions.

I apologise in advance for what I have not been able to fit in, and for people from the church's past who deserved a mention but ended up being left out. And any mistakes you spot are all my own work - don't be afraid to let me know!

Special thanks must go to Giles Liddell who has assisted in many ways, in particular digitising countless photos and documents, unearthing fascinating facts from a myriad of press cuttings going back 200 years and guiding me through the modern technology of computers and how to extract information from the web.

Also, I appreciate Derrick Phillips passing on his experience of self-publishing without which knowledge this book project might never have crossed the finishing line!

Contents

Preface

As the 200th anniversary of the church at Whiteshill approached it was suggested I might write an update of its history, a book having been researched and produced by church member Lettie Fitz 25 years previously.

I was assured that the very early records had been destroyed or lost many years ago, but tidying an old filing cabinet at church I discovered a pile of record books – although incomplete - going back to its formation in 1816.

A few quiet days in the Bristol and the Gloucester record offices unearthed more relevant documents. On top of this the availability these days of so much information 'on line' – in particular copies of 19th Century newspapers, Christian magazines and census returns - provided lots more relevant material on church people and events.

All this sparked my interest in starting from scratch and resulted in a series of short articles – one being handed out with our church news sheet every few weeks throughout the anniversary year. This book is the outcome of putting all these articles together and adding new facts and figures that I have come across since. It focuses predominantly on the early days … because I find that the most fascinating!

As well as ensuring this history is not now lost, I hope the book gives a feel for what has changed – and what hasn't – over 200 years of Christian worship at Whiteshill.

Howard Berry   December 2017

How it all came about

The Whiteshill church building at Hambrook in what is now South Gloucestershire, opened for worship in August 1816 but the history of its congregation goes back to a good three years earlier than that. On 10th April 1813, *'a place of religious worship by protestant dissenters of the independent denomination'* was registered with the Bishop of Gloucester. It was to use the ground floor of a house in Winterbourne occupied at the time by one Henry Tripp.[1]

It does not seem unreasonable to think this was the Henry Tripp recorded in the history of Zion United Church, Frampton Cotterell – the next village to Winterbourne along the turnpike road - as having gone out from that chapel to Jamaica a couple of years later as a missionary. Zion chapel and the fledgling Winterbourne meeting were both under the wing of the Bristol Itinerant Society during the period in question.

When construction of the church at Whiteshill was completed, the Winterbourne congregation transferred into it, as did the Sabbath, or Sunday School which had started sometime in 1814 - probably in the Spring of that year. The Sabbath School had grown to include 40 children and 14

---

[1] *Born in 1784, from 14 years old Tripp served as a sailor on man-of-war ships for seven years before returning to 'the land' and being ordained. From 1815 he spent eight hard years in Jamaica (where his first wife died) as a missionary to the Negros on the sugar plantations. In 1831, with his second wife and children, he sailed to the US where, with other Congregationalists and Presbyterians, a community was founded in the Michigan 'pioneering outback' - as it was in those times. The settlement was called Tripp Town until shortened to Tipton as it is today. The sawmill he built and ran to serve the area's logging trade is now a museum.*

adults. It seems likely this was as many as could be accommodated until it moved from an ordinary dwelling into the more spacious new chapel building, where its numbers soon greatly increased. It is also recorded that a body of dissenting worshippers meeting at Pye Corner, Hambrook, joined with the church at Whiteshill just a little later.

Each of the early gatherings in Winterbourne and Pye Corner was initiated and supported by the Bristol Itinerant Society, an organisation founded in 1811 by a group of wealthy city gentlemen and merchants. They were clearly impressed by the Bristol churches' fervour for sending missionaries to spread the Gospel overseas to the native tribes throughout the British Empire but they saw an equally urgent need to reach 'the heathen at home', as they were not hesitant to describe the occupants of the 'dark' villages beyond the city boundaries.

The Itinerant Society employed dedicated men who were expected, and willing, to walk from Bristol to various villages[2], in all weathers, to preach and organise Sunday Schools in which children, and often some adults, were taught to read using the Bible as their text book. As well as preaching and distributing gospel tracts to local houses, a priority was to set up Sabbath Schools for children, who they saw as being in particular danger from the 'ignorance and vice' in which they were being brought up.

---

[2] As the Itinerant Society tended to focus on villages to the Gloucestershire side of Bristol, when several of Bristol's Baptist ministers set up a similar work in 1817 they concentrated on villages on the Somerset side of the City.

The Society was only too pleased when those attending their *preaching stations* and teaching in the Sunday Schools felt led to set up a local chapel, releasing the itinerant preachers to work in other villages. With a building plot for a chapel being offered at Whiteshill by village land and property owner Joseph Wickwick, the Society actively backed him and other local Christians in their desire to put up a dedicated place of worship.

For many years the Itinerant Society provided the trustees to guide the spiritual direction of the church while leaving the local congregation to manage its day-to-day running. As the original trustees passed on, local church leaders were elected by the congregation to share in the overseeing role by becoming trustees.

The itinerant preachers continued to 'fill the pulpit' at the new church until the local congregation was ready, by the beginning of 1819, to organise ordained ministers from the surrounding area to conduct services – and some of these came by horse rather than walking! Before too long, the church felt ready to seek a full time minister and in 1822, Samuel Weston, who had visited to conduct Sunday services on several occasions accepted the offer to take up the pastorate of the church.

Close links were kept with the Itinerant Society and for a long time Whiteshill turned to their preachers to conduct Sunday services when the church was 'between' ministers. The church came very much under the wing of the Society again for two decades from 1845 when, although very active and launching a day school and evening classes, it had no permanent minister.

What's in a name?

Today the church is called 'Whiteshill Evangelical Church' but that has not always been its name. Each of the three words that make up the current title has altered or changed over the 200 years of its existence.

The location of the church, as with many ancient place names, has been written in different ways over time. In 1816, when the building was erected, it was spelt as two words and with an apostrophe – *White's Hill*. Maps of that era show the same spelling but gradually references to the location dropped the apostrophe. The next change saw the two words sometimes being written as one – as we know it now – until *Whiteshill* became the accepted spelling well before the dawn of the 20th Century.

Take a look at the engraved lettering above what was the entrance to the school from the days when it operated in the rooms at the back of the church. You would be forgiven for thinking that the mid-19th Century  stonemason was not quite decided on whether he should be chiselling out *'WHITES HILL'* or *'WHITESHILL'*. Is that definitely a gap between two words or just the spacing of the lettering gone a bit awry?

In 1958 there was a serious suggestion that it would be better to use the word *'Hambrook'* in place of *'Whiteshill'* in the title of the church. Apparently there had been some confusion when, more than once, visitors trying to find the church ended up at Whites Hill in the St George area of Bristol, several miles from their intended destination. But Whiteshill it stayed!

Whatever way it has been spelt, Whiteshill has always been in the ancient parish of Winterbourne although if you dig back far enough this was variously spelt Wintreborn, Wynterbourne, Winterburn and Winterborn. Even the adjoining hamlet of Pye Corner was once spelt Pie Corner. (I wonder if that denoted an earlier version of a McDonalds fast food outlet serving hungry travellers on the turnpike road that passes by the church!)

As for what District the church is in; that has changed name many times with successive local government re-organisations. Between 1875 and 1895 the area was within the Rural Sanitary Authority of Barton Regis and then within Barton Regis Rural District. That was abolished in favour of Chipping Sodbury Rural District in 1904, being shortened to Sodbury Rural District in 1935.

The creation of Avon County in 1974 saw the parish of Winterbourne become part of the county's Northavon District. It is currently under the South Gloucestershire unitary authority which was formed out of the borough of Kingswood and the district of Northavon, when Avon was disbanded in 1996.

As for the middle word in the church name, which serves to signal the strand of Christian thought or practice with which the church identifies itself, there have been three different ones. The word *'Evangelical'* in the name only goes back to 1970 although it is clear that from its roots onward it has been an evangelical church. God's love for humanity demonstrated in Christ's death and resurrection which secures salvation for those who accept this freely-offered gift has always been at the heart of its beliefs.

The earliest documents call it an *'Independent'* church; a fast growing grouping of nonconformist or dissenting churches at the start of the 19th Century. These were churches that reckoned each individual gathering of Christians should be self-governing before God, without any outside hierarchy or set form of worship imposed on them. The name *'Congregational'* which the church later came to use makes the same point – that the congregation of Christians within the local church would decide on all matters, by seeking God's leading through prayer and applying Bible principles.

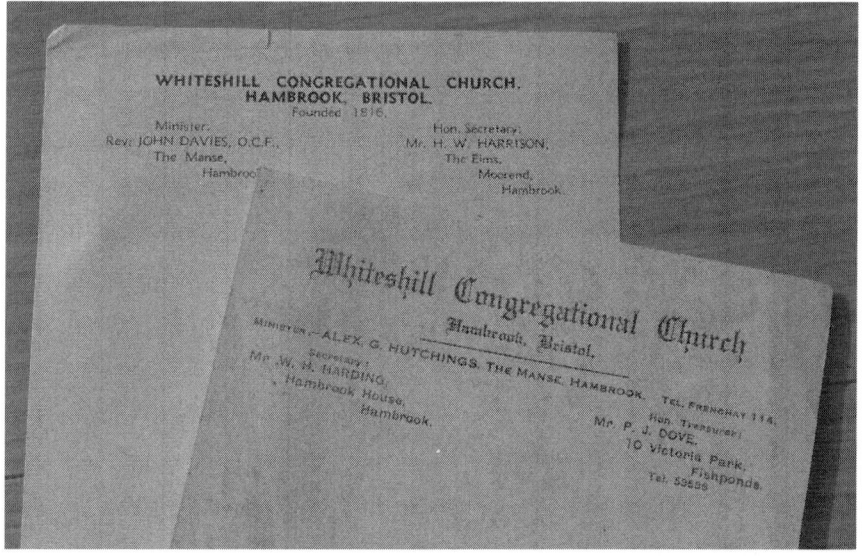

Letterheads bearing the name the church used during the largest part of its history.

In the early 19th Century the words *'Independent'* and *'Congregational'* were interchangeable. Exactly when the word *'Congregational'* appeared on a name board outside the Whiteshill church building we do not know. What we do know is that in the government's religious census of 1851 church deacon Moses Young classified the church as *'Independent.'* On the other hand, as early as 1827 it was included in a listing of Gloucestershire Congregational Churches.

Ten years later, the by then ex-minister of Whiteshill, Samuel Weston, filing his record of White's Hill baptisms with the Commissioners for Non-Parochial Registers, wrote that the church was *'Congregational or Independent'*. That said, on the front page of the record book he lodged with the Commissioners, he states he was *'Minister of The Independent Church at White's Hill in the County of Gloucester'*.

Looking at old maps, by the beginning of the 20th Century it was certainly being shown as a Congregational chapel. It was for many decades very much part of the Gloucestershire and Hereford Congregational Union although its links with the national Congregational Union of England and Wales were more distant.

By 1965 the Congregational Union was looking to unite with the Presbyterian churches in England in what was to become the United Reform Church (URC). To aid the negotiations the Union asked churches to sign up to a covenant which brought in a measure of central control and direction, as opposed to the previous recognition of each Congregational church's complete autonomy. The membership at Whiteshill voted not to sign, thereby breaking its long links with the Congregationalists.

After a query from the Sodbury Rural District Registrar in 1970 about the name of the church, the church decided to adopt its current title – *Whiteshill Evangelical Church*. It had already joined the Evangelical Alliance and at the end of 1978 applied for affiliation to the Fellowship of Independent Evangelical Churches (FIEC), being accepted the following July. In 1982 the FIEC was asked, and accepted being the holding trustees for both the church and the manse with the church officers as the managing trustees.

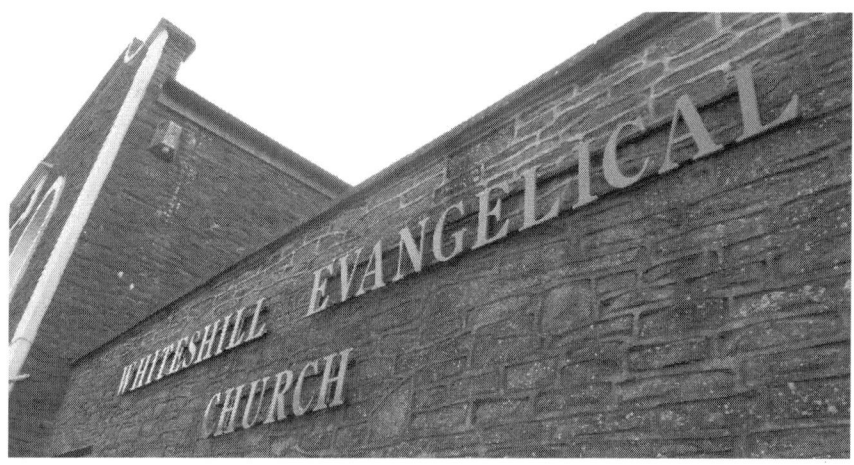

As for the third word in the church name, in the 1816 deeds it is simply referred to as a *'Meeting Place'* and a *'Place of Public Religious Worship for the Service of Almighty God'* – very good but a bit long for a church name! It was soon being called a chapel, no doubt to differentiate itself from the established Church of England, and right through to this day is upon occasion referred to as such. Today it is officially titled a church although its congregation, without doubt, would feel that the Christian people who meet in the building are really 'The Church' and not the 200 years old structure in which they gather for worship.

Tolerated but not always accepted

Nathaniel Good, Joseph Wickwick and the other founding fathers of the church at Whiteshill lodged a *'certificate'* dated 7th August 1816 with the office of the Bishop of Gloucester informing him that *'a certain meeting place situate at White's Hill is to be used as a place of religious worship'*. It might seem to be a sign of politeness to let the Church of England authorities know that a nonconformist church was to be opened a couple of weeks later in the County.

In fact, far from a matter of courteousness, the letter to the recently appointed Bishop of Gloucester, Dr Henry Ryder, was only sent to meet a legal requirement. Any new 'dissenting' place of worship had by law to register with the very organisation from which it was breaking free!

Persecution and prosecution of those refusing to recognise and worship under the rites and rules of the country's established church – the Church of England – had been officially brought to an end more than a century earlier through the 1689 Act of Toleration. However, the Act still placed limitations on religious equality for nonconformists and their meeting places, and many of these restrictions remained in force over 120 years later when the chapel at Whiteshill was founded.

King William III and Queen Mary's Act of Toleration meant dissenters were no longer compelled to attend Church of England services but that freedom had its limits. Previously, non-attendance could incur a penalty of 12 pence a time or a term in prison if the fine could not be paid. From 1689 dissenters were at liberty to meet together for worship with their own teachers and preachers, subject to swearing an oath of allegiance to the Crown and their places of worship being registered. Roman Catholics and Unitarians had to wait far longer before they were granted the same freedom.

By the start of the 19th Century, the Anglican church, both houses of parliament and many of the gentry were deeply suspicious, and concerned for the social order, as they witnessed more and more new chapels springing up across the country.

Frightened by what they had seen happen across the Channel after the French Revolution, lobbied by High Churchmen, and fearing that education might arouse demands for increased freedom, in 1801 the Pitt government actually contemplated bringing in a Bill for *'suppressing all Sunday Schools and all village preaching'*. Rowland Hill, who preached at the opening of the church at Whiteshill was one of the leaders in stopping that particular Bill becoming law.

Over the first few years of its existence, there are reports of smashed windows at Whiteshill chapel. One of several similar entries in the Accounts Book reads, '*... for work done in and about said Chapel, including £1/17/- cash paid, when the Windows was broke, 12th March 1821'*. What other, if any, physical attacks on the building or disruption of services were encountered we do not know but such incidents were far from unknown at dissenting chapels in this era.

Forsaking the Anglicans in favour of the independent church at Whiteshill when it was first built, would not have been a step to be taken lightly or without strong conviction.

That said, there was not always antagonism between 'Church and Chapel'; indeed in some towns and cities evangelical Church of England and nonconformist ministers worked together to reach local communities with the Gospel and to support overseas missionary work. But often, at best, they kept themselves to themselves. A rector of Winterbourne parish church wrote of his 1830s predecessor, William Birkett Allen, that he was a *'sworn foe of all dissenters, and that it was no good for a chapel-goer to ask him for anything'*.

In a clear attack on the nonconformists, there was an outcry when in 1810 Lord Sidmouth introduced a Bill in parliament to *'restrict the liberty which persons enjoyed of becoming preachers of the Christian Religion'*. Very brief notice was given of the second reading of the Bill but in just 48 hours, 336 petitions arrived from congregations within reach of London opposing what would have put a stop to much itinerant preaching. Not only was the Bill thrown out but, backfiring on the intentions of its supporters, the episode galvanised support to campaign for the end of many legal restrictions that could still be evoked 120 years after the Act of Toleration.

Nevertheless, it took until 1832, for an Act of Parliament to do away with the requirement for anyone holding civil office – such as mayors, MPs and members of the House of Lords, or those holding military rank, to be taking Communion *'in accordance with the rites of the Church of England'*.

Only in 1871 did Parliament repeal the Act that had, until then, barred nonconformists from the top universities - Durham, Oxford and Cambridge. Even after that, university professors had to be Anglicans and this ban on nonconformists was only lifted just three years before the church at Whiteshill celebrated its centenary.

The Church of England alone could conduct marriages at the time Whiteshill opened and this was the situation for the following two decades. It was in 1836 that the Anglican marriage monopoly ended, after which other religious groups could register their buildings, permitting their ministers to conduct weddings as long as a Registrar and two witnesses were present.

Although nonconformists gradually won the right to take their place in society like any other citizen, they had one major grievance which took a very long time to settle. Leaving the Church of England did not give any exemption from paying a tithe or church rate to fund its clergy and build its churches.

A hard fought battle took until 1868 to achieve the abolition of the compulsory payment of the church rate. So, for its first 50 years, members of Whiteshill had to bear all the costs of running their own church and employing a minister, while at the same time being forced to pay towards the expenses of the Church of England.

Buying the land and constituting a church

First buy a plot of land and then put up the building. That would seem the normal way of doing things, but in the case of the church at Whiteshill it happened the other way round. The construction of the building was well advanced before ownership of the land passed over from Joseph Wickwick to the newly appointed trustees of the church.

Wickwick owned the dozen or so houses (long since demolished) and fields running down the hill between Whiteshill House and the White Horse public house. In 1798, he had bought Whiteshill House which included ten acres of grounds, in part of which the chapel came to be built. Its previous owner, surgeon Dr Thomas Mountjoy[3], had died the year before. Wickwick lived nearby but rented out this particular property.

Keen to see a dissenter's chapel in the locality, he allowed building work to get underway long before legal ownership of the plot of land was transferred to the church trustees on 14th June 1816. This was less than ten weeks prior to the building being completed and in full use on its 49 feet by 88

---

[3] *Dr Mountjoy had been falsely accused in 1768 of dissecting, at Whiteshill House, the body of a murdered Negro servant of Captain John Read of Frenchay. The house had long associations with doctors or surgeons. It was occupied by surgeon Robert Alloway at the time the chapel was built and later by a Dr John Hay. After his death in 1856, it was bought by his partner Dr Edward Crossman.*

feet (15m x 27m) piece of land fronting onto the turnpike road.

The title deed, in those days called an indenture, runs to over 5,000 words with not a single full stop or any other punctuation throughout the three large sheets of ornately-

Just one corner of one page of the lengthy and convoluted wording of the 1816 chapel deeds.

penned parchment. It is known that lawyers and their clerks were sometimes paid in proportion to the length of the deeds they were required to draft, but this was not the only reason why this one turned out to be so very wordy.

As well as there being 13 church trustees to be named at numerous points in the agreement, the document doubled up as the trust deed for the church. Then there was one more complication it had to address.

Three years earlier Wickwick had married Joanna Hale. A matter of days before the wedding took place on 23rd March 1813, maybe because neither were youngsters at the time, Joseph had signed a marriage settlement [4] involving trustees. This would have been to ensure Joanna had the benefit of the land and property should he die before her, as back then she would not have been able to own them in her own right.

So when the Wickwicks wanted to give up even a relatively small part of the grounds of Whiteshill House for the chapel building, the marriage settlement trustees – two Bristol lawyers, one of whom went on to be the City's Lord Mayor in 1843 – had to be party to the written agreement, giving consent to the sale.

The section of the indenture document that constitutes the church deeds lays down the basic purpose and organisation of the church; to be '… *peaceably used occupied and enjoyed as a place of public Religious Worship for the Service of Almighty God by the Society of Protestant Dissenters of the denomination usually called Calvinistic Independants* [sic] *within and about the Parish of Winterbourne …'*.

The indenture specified that the church minister was to be chosen by the trustees with the agreement of the majority of the men and women who had taken Communion at the meeting house for at least six months. Should the number of trustees drop to five then extra trustees were to be appointed to bring the number back up to 13, with the

---

[4] *In the event, the settlement was not needed as Joanna died first, in 1817 aged only 52, after just four and a half years of marriage, with Joseph living on until 1831 when he died at the age of 70.*

consent of the majority of the remaining trustees and with the agreement of the majority of the communicants.

The original trustees were from the Bristol Itinerant Society. Over the decades, as trustees died, ensuring the number did not drop below five became a recurring problem – with the possibility of the Charity Commission appointing trustees whether members agreed to the names or not.

A solution to the problem was found 35 years ago by appointing the Fellowship of Independent Evangelical Churches (FIEC Ltd) as the holding trustees with the church officers - deacons and pastor - being the managing trustees, thereby continuing the independence of the local church.

Getting back to 1816, one of the grievances of dissenters at that time was the considerable cost incurred in being required to have deeds drawn up when founding a chapel. Incorporating them in the title deeds of the land must have represented a useful cost-saving for the fledgling church at Whiteshill.

The details are hard to fathom from the deed document even with the help of the 1816 church accounts. They record that Joseph Wickwick received £22/10/0 for the plot of land but fees and legal expenses doubled the amount that had to be paid by the church. Costs included a fee for 'enrolling' or registering ownership of the land through the law courts, as needed to be done prior to the Land Registry being created 45 years later.

When one considers that the annual rental value of a very 'up-market' house in rural 1816 was no more than £10, it is easy to see why legal costs of several times that amount were a particularly unwelcome burden for chapel founders.

It was reckoned at the time that the cost of preparing chapel trust deeds was between £30 and £40, with up to as much again each time the deeds were revised with changes of trustees. Clearly, in the case of Whiteshill the cost was significantly lower.

Of the £22/10/0 for which Wickwick sold the land he passed back £10 towards the cost of building the chapel. And when the church started paying a full-time minister in the 1820s Wickwick made several special donations of £1 or one guinea [£1/1/0] to help balance the books.

Typical early 19th Century chapel building

In the early 19th Century, chapels were being erected in great numbers up and down the country. In Gloucestershire alone the amount of nonconformist chapel buildings nearly doubled between 1812 and 1827 – from 36 to 70. Architects were known to look at recently-built chapels and then reflect that style in their own work, resulting in many similarities in chapel design.

The 'golden rule' was to keep it simple, both outside and inside. *'Chaste and beautiful'* design was considered to befit the simplicity of worship sought by the dissenting congregations. The grander High Classical and ornate Gothic design of nonconformist chapels and churches only became prevalent from the 1850s, decades after Whiteshill was built.

The description of the building given by English Heritage when it was given Grade ll listing in 1984 reads: *Chapel. Rubble, freestone dressings, concrete and clay double roman tile roofs. Single storey chapel is 2 windows wide, 2 deep, all tall round-headed multi-pane sashes, those on entrance front have architraves, between them a plain door and porch with unadorned cornice, above is date-stone under cornice; end pilaster strips rise to low coped parapet which sweeps up to conceal most of hipped roof.*

I wonder how different we would find the church building of 1816 compared to the one worshiped in today. Let's start by going through the wrought iron gates between the pavement and the church lawn. There would have been no pavement, nor come to that a well made-up road in 1816, but the gates are reckoned to be original, supplied by a Mr Gay at a cost of five guineas [£5/5/0] – although it was not too far short of another 150 years before the decorative metal arch holding a lamp over the top of the gates was added.

Original gates and pillars, but with overhead lamp not
added until around the end of the 1950s.

To begin with, between the front gates and the front of the church was rough ground, probably with trees remaining from before the plot was built upon. A year later, it was thanks to the caretaker, James Cole and his wheel barrow, that stone and gravel were hauled in, laid and levelled.

The front boundary wall was higher then and not reduced to its present height until 1966, to make the church more visible. In fact, the building of stables (now a house) close to the road in much earlier times, by then next-door neighbour Dr Crossman, stopped the church being as visually dominant on the top of the hill as it had been originally.

Also more visible before the stables were built would have been the Bristol Union plaque or 'firemark' high up on the side wall facing the road to Bristol – along which, it was to be hoped, that particular insurance company's horse-drawn fire engine crew would have arrived in time to deal with any outbreak of fire.[5]

How the firemark would have looked when first fixed up…and how it looks now!

Looking up at the front of the chapel today, outwardly it is almost entirely unaltered, even down to the thin glass in the windows! The one difference since 1816 is that the original doors have gone - but not the surround - and in their place

---

[5] *Local government (outside the Capital) did not become responsible for providing a Fire Service until the late 19th Century. When Whiteshill chapel was built insurance companies each had their own fire engines and only tackled fires in premises displaying their company's firemark. The chapel has a 'Bristol Union' plaque (its wording now hardly legible) – the firemark of the Bristol Union Fire & Life Insurance Company, which existed from 1818 to 1844.*

is a window looking into the main worship area, with the entrance now through the 1980s extension, set slightly back to the side of the building.

In the days when the entrance doors were in the front of the building, there was a very small lobby directly inside, with doors in it to either side. These led to a further door each side through to the church, plus doors to a cloakroom on one side (in later years a recording room) and to the balcony stairs on the other. All these doors and partitions were removed once the current main entrance came into use, save for the lower part of the cloakroom partition which now screens the desk used for sound and computer projection equipment.

Besides the chapel itself, the original premises only included a vestry - no more than ten feet long and seven feet wide [3m x 2.1m] but with its own fireplace in one corner - a coal house and 'other offices', a term usually meaning toilets! The vestry was attached to the right hand side of the church with a door through into the main building. The toilets, or probably just one toilet, would have been somewhere outside. Inside toilets were frowned upon – just as well at Whiteshill, as even cesspit drainage was not installed until 1880 and water not piped in until ten years after that!

The little vestry was lengthened and altered over the years to accommodate indoor toilets and a kitchen. All these were completely demolished in 1986 to make way for the current much larger side extension housing entrance foyer, toilets, boiler-house, kitchen, vestry and another small meeting room. The extension was officially opened in May 1991.

The two-storey structure attached to the back of the chapel is a product of the very beginning of the 1860s, added to house a day school set up by the church members. It used up every last square inch of spare ground to the back of the plot of land that had been bought in 1816.

Volunteers knock down the 1816 vestry – the only part of the original structure that no longer exists.

Moving inside, differences between the original interior and that of today would be immediately noticeable. In 1816 the pulpit rose much higher, flanked on either side by arched windows, with no organ, or other musical instrument to be seen. The pair of windows, similar in size to those in the other three walls of the chapel, had to be blocked up when the school rooms were grafted onto the back of the building in the mid-19th Century.

Rarely if ever used in today's services, the pulpit is the same one that was installed when the church was built but it was lowered onto a rostrum in the 1870s. This was at around the same time as the layout of the pews was altered or, more likely, the original pews replaced. The pulpit, doubtless the oldest feature of the Whiteshill church, was given by the friends at Castle Green Chapel in Bristol when their church was rebuilt in 1815 to accommodate its swelling congregation. The only cost for the pulpit was the £1 paid to have it *'hauled'* by horse and cart from Bristol.

As well as the balcony we know today, there was at least one raised area of seating, partitioned off from the rest of the pews, for the family of Hannah Walters and her husband Howell, who was a school master occupying Victoria Lodge in affluent Frenchay. Mr Walters paid three guineas [£3/3/0] a year for their privileged seating arrangement and sometimes paid separately to rent seats in the main pews for some of his pupils.

We do not know the colour the interior walls were first painted[6] but the doors and woodwork were 'white lime' waxed – to whiten and highlight the grain of the bare wood.

Attending a winter evening service in 1816 would have revealed two of the biggest differences from today. The church would have been lit entirely by candles – and not

---

[6] *The pulpit decoration was increased using black cloth edged with black fringing nine months after the chapel opened but 'the Table' – presumably the Communion table - was covered with green cloth. That might point to the walls being green. For sure, in later years the interior walls were painted and repainted green.*

just for a carol service as happens today! - and heating was provided by a coal fire.

The Bristol men behind founding the chapel

A look at the people behind establishing the chapel at Whiteshill in 1816 gives an insight into a time when Bristol, with its thriving port, was one of the country's premier hubs for world trade. The construction of the chapel in 1816 was underwritten by the Bristol Itinerant Society, whose members, alongside being strongly committed to spreading the Gospel at home and overseas, were, in the main, wealthy city merchants.

The stated professions of the 13 founding trustees, each nominated by the Itinerant Society and all residing in Bristol, give a snapshot of the trade that was securing and supporting the prosperity of the rapidly growing city in the early years of the 19th Century - woollen draper; tobacconist; hatter, brush maker, grocer, dry-salter [7], shoemaker, clockmaker, carpenter.

Some of these might seem like very ordinary jobs – but in fact most of these men were running international businesses, involving the import of raw materials and the export far and wide of finished products. One of the trustees was listed as a 'gentleman', indicating the higher social standing of someone who, through inherited wealth and land ownership, did not see it as necessary nor desirable to engage personally in any trade or business.

---

[7] *A dry-salter dealt primarily in chemical products including glues, varnish, dye, colourings and salt for preserving food.*

The merchants were bringing prosperity to the city but there were ups and downs along the way and many ordinary people, of course, were not touched by the considerable wealth being generated. In 1816 and over the following few years, the business community and the population in general felt the effect of government efforts to re-stabilise the British currency and manage the high level of the national debt caused by the heavy expense of the war with France, which had ended with Napoleon's final defeat at the Battle of Waterloo the previous year.

Andrew Pope, the first of the trustees to be listed on the 1816 church deeds soon featured in one of the major setbacks suffered by the city. From a well-respected and wealthy merchant family, his father had been Sheriff and then Mayor of the city. Andrew Pope had taken his turn at being Master of the Merchant Venturers, the society that until 1848 was the all-important port authority.

He was a manager of the Bristol Tabernacle in Penn Street, one of the three large nonconformist city churches who were the principal supporters of the Itinerant Society; the other two being Castle Green and Bridge Street Independent chapels.

Pope was a prominent banker, founding in 1808 with two others, the banknote-issuing Bristol Tolzey Bank and was engaged in various philanthropic activities. Dramatically, in 1819 his private bank failed. The 'Annals of Bristol' record that *'great consternation was caused in the city and the neighbourhood by the failure. Though of recent origin the bank had issued a great number of notes for 20/- and 30/- each, and the disaster hit all classes in the locality and caused a run on some of the other banks, then eleven in number'.*

It is no surprise that the now bankrupt Andrew Pope is missing from the list of trustees signing a church document at the end of that same year. The second signatory of the deeds, Richard Ash, has a happier story. Ash, the one trustee listed as a *'gentleman'*, had a long record as a *'munificent benefactor of so many Bristol institutions'*.

He was involved in many charities and served on the Bristol town council. Ash laid the foundation stone of a number of new Independent or Congregational churches in Bristol including the Redland Park and Arley chapels, and was a major financial contributor to both.

In the early 1840s he bought a £280 plot of ground across the road from his 'Cotham House' mansion and gave it for the building of a place of worship *'in the independent or congregational connexion'* to serve the new residential district of Cotham that had started to be developed in the previous few years. This was Highbury Chapel[8] at the top of St Michael's Hill, in Bristol.

The Whiteshill trustee who signed himself as a tobacconist; Samuel Ditchett, was the partner (and brother-in-law) of Henry Overton Wills in the tobacco manufacturing firm, Wills & Ditchett, formed in 1803 – better known as W D & H O Wills after Ditchett retired from the company in 1830.

---

[8] *The 700-seat Highbury chapel became Bristol's foremost Congregational church. An early work of William Butterfield, one of the foremost ecclesiastical architects of the 19th Century, its Gothic Revival style departed from traditional nonconformist architecture. A nephew of Congregationalist W D Wills, Butterfield was himself a high churchman and went on to design over 60 Anglican chapels, churches and cathedrals. In 1972 the chapel closed as a Congregational church and today is the Church of England's Cotham parish church.*

Ditchett was president of 'The Grateful Society' in 1817, a charity involved in care of the elderly and later was Governor of the 'Asylum for the support and education of the Deaf and Dumb Children of the Poor'.

Wills and Ditchett were staunch Congregationalists and although not himself a trustee of the church, H O Wills (the first of three 'H O Wills') signed off one of the early church accounts and had contributed to the building costs – as had the Wills & Ditchett company. H O Wills ll (or was it lll?) was appointed a trustee of the church in 1856 when those who had by then died were replaced. H O Wills lll – the first Chancellor of Bristol University - was a trustee of the first Whiteshill church manse when it was bought in 1909.

Of John Holmes, another original and long-serving trustee, we know little detail other than that he was a *'merchant'*. Obviously wanting to keep his good deeds to between his God and himself it was written of him that he gave *'lavish gifts to Bristol ... sometimes disguised as from Aged Christian'*.

The most intriguing trustee was Samuel Blackwell, a lay preacher and ardent anti-slavery campaigner. Listed in the deeds as a grocer, a little later he was the owner of a sugar refinery. This he sold and emigrated to America in 1831 taking with him his pregnant wife Hannah, their eight children, a governess, two servants and three of his four sisters.

His determination that his daughters were given as good an education as his sons was rewarded when two of them went on to be pioneering physicians. Elizabeth became the first woman to qualify as a doctor in the United States and the first to practice medicine. Emily was only the third female graduate of a US medical school. But Samuel did not live to see his children's success, dying of malaria in 1838.

Trustees Thomas Farrington (clockmaker), Samuel Wade (brush and bellows maker), Joseph Rider (shoe maker) and John Evans (hatter) would have undoubtedly been wealthy but probably not in quite the same league of super-rich merchants judging by their smaller, but still worthy contributions to the chapel building costs.

The son of trustee Samuel Jackson (accountant and later dry-salter) is better known in the history of the city than his father. Samuel Jackson junior, a landscape watercolourist and oil painter was credited with being the *father of the Bristol school of Artists'* in the 1820s.

Finally, two trustees, Richard Hemsley and his brother-in-law John Godwin, together owned an extensive woollen drapery business. Based in Castle Street but also operating elsewhere, it traded under their names - 'Godwin & Hemsley'. Godwin was one of the Bristol Itinerant Society founders and the church at Whiteshill came to owe him a debt of gratitude resulting in a plaque which still hangs on the wall inside the church.

A 'home' for local worshippers

The chapel trustees were not 'locals' but the first worshippers certainly were, and several generations of quite a few of Whiteshill chapel's 1816 congregation stayed living in the locality - as most people did in those days - and remained active in the church down through the years. The 'Goods' and the 'Pendocks' are prime examples.

In 1816 the responsibility for constructing the building fell primarily on the shoulders of local man Nathaniel Good who went on to be chapel manager and its first treasurer. For the following one-and-a-quarter centuries his children, grandchildren, great-grandchildren and even great-great-grandchildren, featured in the life of the chapel – the family name not disappearing from the records until the death in 1941 of Clara Elizabeth Good, a church member of over 50 years standing, who had run the village store in Hambrook,

Long-time church member Clara Good ran the Hambrook grocery shop and before her it was in the hands of her mother Elizabeth.

having taken it over from her widowed mother Elizabeth Good. (After Clara retired the shop was enlarged and run by the Harrisons for ten years and then by the Braceys until 1960. Both these couples were Whiteshill chapel members, H W Harrison serving as church secretary for some years.)

The 'early' Goods were a prosperous land and property-owning family of some standing in the locality[9] although nowhere near as well off as the Bristol merchants who underwrote the cost of building the chapel. Country families such as the Goods or the Pendocks might have one, or at best two live-in servants, but could not match the six, seven or more, employed by those in the City of Bristol's higher social classes.

Nathaniel and his wife Hester, nee King (another chapel founding family, from Frenchay) had more than ten children although, far from uncommon in those days, at least four died in infancy, another in his 'teens' and two more in their forties.

Their surviving children were baptised in the parish church but for some reason, in 'batches' as teenagers or even older; not as infants. One son was baptised on the day of his

---

[9] *Nathaniel Good's son George was the 1841 Census Enumerator for Hambrook, responsible for listing details of all those living in the district in the first population census to be carried out at the same time throughout the country. He was also the deputy district registrar of births and deaths. Another son, Nathaniel (junior), was appointed to be one of two 'collectors of the Monies' due from 'the Tything of Hambrook' under the 1829 Land Tax assessment and by 1831 was joint local assessor of personal taxes. Even back then tax assessment was not easy, with complicated rules about what tax was to be levied on horses, on carriages, on people using hair powder and although window tax had generally stopped it was still applied if a property had more than eight windows – and these were just a few of the taxes detailed in the instructions issued to Nathaniel.*

marriage, maybe to placate the parish church in which the ceremony was to take place.

All Nathaniel Good's children were born many years before he had the opportunity – in his early sixties - to oversee the building of *a place of public Religious Worship'* in his own village where his and other dissenting families could meet together to hold services. A carpenter by training, Nathaniel, by the time the chapel was built, was more likely a builder employing a number of men.

Almost £350 - half the cost of building the chapel once the land purchase and legal expenses are stripped out, went through Nathaniel's hands, to pay either his own men, or additional tradesmen he employed on the building work. Other major bills were from Thomas Mitchell, a local stonemason, Mr Monks a quarryman and from the *'tylers'* – accounting for the walls and the roof tiling of the building.

Smaller invoices came from a *'glasier'* and a *'brazier'*, plus £4/14/0 for a *'Dial'* - a clock which needed much attention over the years - and five guineas [£5/5/0] for the *'Iron Gates'* which are thought to be the ones still standing at the pedestrian entrance to the church grounds. Finally there was a bill of a little under £2 for *'Velvet and Trimmings'* supplied by a Mrs Foster to provide a minimum of decorative ornamentation for the chapel interior, primarily to adorn the top of the pulpit lectern.

Nathaniel died 12 years after the chapel was built and was buried in the Presbyterian chapel cemetery in Frenchay (in the days before it became Unitarian). His wife, Hester, was also laid to rest there three years later.

Their son George[10], who followed in his father's footsteps as a carpenter and builder, carried out maintenance work on the chapel, certainly upon occasion at his own cost. Another son, who had the same Christian name as his father, took over the 18th Century bakehouse in Hambrook with his brother-in-law, Thomas Parker.[11]

It (and the adjoining Post Office) stayed in the family's hands for three generations – until in 1936 Sydney and Bertha Good retired and moved away from the district. Even after this, the bakery continued to give the bread rolls for the Sunday School outings and a harvest loaf each year.[12]

Sydney, Bertha and their three daughters were heavily involved in all aspects of chapel life. Sydney served as a church trustee, a deacon and stood in as church secretary for a time when the office-holder became ill. His daughters, Gertrude, Gwendoline and Irene, took a keen interest in activities for the children and young people of the church. Irene trained and qualified as a nurse before serving as a medical missionary.

---

[10] *Intriguingly, George was christened 'Doctor George'. There was a tradition that the seventh son of a seventh son had 'second sight' or special healing powers hence they were sometimes given the honorary title of 'doctor'. It is certainly possible that George was a seventh son of a seventh son but it is very unlikely that the Goods would have given credence to that meaning he would have such powers.*

[11] *The wives of the two bakers each had a baby in 1830 and had the two children baptised at the same service – each giving their baby daughter the Christian name of the other mother!*

[12] *The Hambrook bakery and adjoining Post Office are today a private house – aptly named 'The Old Bakery' - and a micro-brewery.*

'Pendock' is another family name with a strong Whiteshill church connection – and a name still well known in Hambrook village to this day. Young farmer Jonathan Pendock (later the local High Constable) rented seats at the chapel as soon as it was built in 1816 and was one of the 19 men and women, along with the Goods, who put their names to the document marking the start of formal chapel membership in 1820.

Members of successive generations of Pendocks served the church as enthusiastic members, deacons and trustees, guiding the fellowship in spiritual matters and providing financial, practical and professional help in maintaining the building. Jonathan Pendock's granddaughter Martha was teacher of the infant children in the church's day school and her older sister married the headmaster!

While some of Jonathan Pendock's descendants continued farming at the nearby 200 to 300 acre Harcombe Hill Farm others branched out into carpentry, decorating, house building and undertaking - the local funeral directors' still bearing the name T B and H Pendock. The church's link with the Pendock name ended after more than 160 years when, in the 1980s, Harold Pendock stood down as a church trustee.

With 19th Century village life very much revolving around activities at the chapel and opportunity to travel further afield very limited, it is no surprise that many young people sought and found their spouse from within the congregation. The Goods and the Pendocks were no exception, with Thomas Bridgman Pendock marrying Mary Ann Good[13] at the chapel in 1877.

Marrying 'within the chapel' remained common amongst the congregation well into the 20th Century. In 1936 for instance, Gwendoline Good wed Harold Pendock, forming another link between these two Whiteshill chapel families. Even today, a number of long-standing members of the congregation are distantly related to each other through the many marriages between 'chapel families' in times past.

---

[13] *Mary Ann died after only three years of marriage and widower Thomas Bridgman Pendock, spent the rest of his life boarding in, and running his successful building business from, the living accommodation adjoining Mary's mother, Elizabeth Good's, village store (later run by her daughter Clara). He was also an active member of the rural district council.*

Meeting the building costs

In the enthusiasm of nonconformists to erect new places of worship in the early 19th Century it was common for rural chapels to have building debts hanging over them for many, many years. All too often country ministers had to resort to *'pastoral begging'*; going to preach at town or city churches to solicit donations towards paying off such debt.

It might seem surprising but the wish to regulate this often embarrassing practice was, in the late 1820s, one of the drivers for the formation of a Congregational union.

In the case of Whiteshill, the trustees and other local Christians contributed generously to the £734 cost of building the chapel, meeting almost half the expenditure. The Bristol Itinerary Society itself made a £50 donation and members of the congregation gave what they could.

A collection taken up at the opening of the chapel in August 1816 raised just short of £50 towards the remaining debt. Collections at the anniversary services of 1817, 1818 and 1819 (years of bad harvests and continuing economic difficulty) raised only a further £36. So, four years after construction of the chapel had been completed, £210/4/11 was still owing to the Itinerant Society.

The society's treasurer was John Godwin, a woollen draper living in Cotham and one of the founding trustees of the church. He had a special affection for the church at Whiteshill having been born locally. His mother was Martha Godwin and a person of that name rented a seat at the chapel from when it opened until late in 1820 so that might have given him a special family link to the chapel. Along with his wife, Mary, Godwin had already contributed over £100 towards the cost of building the chapel in addition to regularly subscribing £10 to £15 per annum to its running costs.

Imagine how relieved the congregation was when, at a special meeting in the church vestry on 29th March 1821, chapel manager Nathaniel Good brought the offer from Godwin that if they would pay the sum of £10/4/11 he would write off the remaining £200, *'to be considered by the members and subscribers, as a free Gift from his Children'* – of which he had six at the time!

There and then at the meeting, more than 15 men and women promised amounts that totalled to one penny more than the required amount, allowing the *'very handsome and liberal offer'* from Godwin to be immediately and gratefully taken up.

Godwin's family connection with the chapel extended beyond his brother-in-law Richard Hemsley being a fellow trustee when, in 1848, his daughter, Martha, married Joseph, son of another one of the original trustees, John Foster.

The Fosters, both listed as carpenters, were each heartily commended for their outstanding service to the Itinerant Society. Carpenters by training they may have been, but the Fosters developed a substantial building and contracting business, employing 150 men and ten boys by the 1870s and by the 1880s Joseph was an architect and surveyor.

The Godwin family connection with Whiteshill chapel strengthened further when new trustees were needed in 1856 to replace some who had died over the course of the preceding 40 years. Woollen drapers like their father, two of John Godwin's sons, Christopher and Joseph, were appointed, along with his son-in-law Joseph Foster.

Aside from being a Whiteshill trustee, Christopher Godwin had chaired the building committee for Arley Chapel – for which Joseph Foster was one of the chief promoters. Christopher then became treasurer of Highbury Chapel in 1866 in succession to H O Wills ll.

The one plaque on the church wall is in memory of John Godwin - the largest contributor to the cost of the building.

Upon the death of John Godwin the congregation readily donated the £5/14/0 needed to provide the marble tablet that hangs inside the church, bearing the inscription: *'In memory of the late Mr John Godwin of Cotham near Bristol. He was a native of this parish & in the spiritual welfare of its inhabitants he always took a lively interest. Through his instrumentality and largely by his liberality this place of worship was erected. He departed this life July 4th 1858 aged 82 years.'*

Celebrity opening for the chapel

The church building was completed on time for the planned inaugural services on Wednesday 28th August 1816. Some extra work had been added to the task after building began, possibly the addition of the small vestry on the side, but nevertheless all the construction work had been finished in time.

There was work to do to the ground in front of the new chapel and a few doors needed easing to stop them sticking but that could all wait until after the Big Day.

Well known preachers from out of the area – the celebrities of their day - would be preaching, so the church was sure to be packed. Jane Cole, a member of a chapel-family from its beginnings - more than likely having attended local cottage services that moved into the chapel when it opened - had spent much time cleaning up after the builders finished their work.

A famous preacher from Surrey, Rev Rowland Hill[14], was to give the first sermon in the building. As well as being a

---

[14] *Rowland Hill's 1000+ seat church, Surrey Chapel, was in what is now Southwark. Built for him in 1783, it was surrounded by fields and within the boundary of Surrey. Each summer he undertook itinerant preaching in various places but also spent time in a house at Wotton-under-Edge in Gloucestershire. He became acquainted with Dr Jenner., who lived nearby and Hill became an early champion for vaccination. He set up one of the most effective vaccine boards in London at Surrey Chapel. Wherever he was preaching over the summer, he took to announcing after his sermon, "I am ready to vaccinate to-morrow morning as many children as you choose; and if wish them to escape that horrid disease, the small-pox, you will bring them".*

respected preacher of the Word of God he was known to *'have a great intolerance of dirt and slovenliness.'*

Hill was a 'disciple' of the renowned 18th Century open air preacher and evangelist George Whitefield who is reported to have often used the maxim, *'Cleanliness is next to Godliness'* – and meant it. So the new chapel had to be spick and span throughout, ready for when the first congregations gathered.

The 'opening' preacher,
Rev Rowland Hill

And gather they did! Hill preached first, in the morning. Rev John Liefchild, another notable preacher, from Kensington in London, who a few years later moved to Bristol to become minister of the city's Bridge Street Independent chapel, spoke in the afternoon. Then in the evening it was the turn of Bristol's most well-known Congregationalist, the Rev William Thorpe, minister of Castle Green Independent chapel. Two other London ministers, Rev J Raban and Rev A Tidman made the long journey from the Capital and were *'engaged in the devotional parts of the services'*.

The 1816 Evangelical Magazine & Missionary Chronicle, of which several of the notable ministers present were trustees, reported that on, *'Aug. 28, was opened, at*

Whiteshill[15], near Bristol, a neat chapel, capable of seating 450 persons'. It is doubtless true that the original pew layout would have seated many more people than today's 150-person capacity, but still nowhere near as many as the magazine claimed. In 1851 the church itself estimated it was capable of seating 360 people; a more realistic, if still seemingly very high figure by today's expectation of leg room and elbow space!

From a reliable eye-witness account it is known that the chapel was absolutely full with as many people again having to stand outside. So, in all probability the seating capacity of 450 is a misreporting of the estimated total number present – both in the building and outside.

Standing outside on a sunny August day might seem quite pleasant, until you remember that the year of 1816 has gone down in history as, *'The Year without a Summer'* [16], caused by the devastating climatic effects of several volcanic eruptions, culminating in the 1815 eruption of Mount Tambora in the Dutch East Indies (now Indonesia) – the world's largest eruption for at least 1,300 years.

Whatever the weather might have been, Hill, considered somewhat of an eccentric by the standards of his day,

---

[15] *A mistake at the time, the publication spelt 'Whiteshill' as one word and without the apostrophe!*

[16] *'The year without a summer' was an unprecedented global agricultural disaster, particularly severe across swathes of North America and Western Europe. Cool temperatures and heavy rains resulted in failed harvests in Britain and Ireland for several years. Families in Wales travelled long distances as refugees, begging for food. Famine was prevalent in North and Southwest Ireland, following crop failure. Still recuperating from the Napoleonic Wars, food riots broke out in the UK and France, and grain warehouses were looted. The death rate doubled in 1816.*

decided to preach from the balcony with the windows open, so that those outside would not lose the benefit of his sermon. In its short article on the opening, the Evangelical Magazine sums up the day as follows, *'the congregations were very numerous and attentive, and liberal collections were made'*.

Up and running

On the first Sunday of September 1816 - a week-and-a-half after the Wednesday of the chapel opening - 'normal' worship services and Sabbath School commenced in the new building. Worshippers and Sabbath School pupils transferred from their 'cottage meeting' venue in Winterbourne to the new premises, to be joined later by other Christians who had previously gathered for worship at a dwelling in Pye Corner.

Sunday services were held at 10.30am and in the evening - as far as we know at 6pm. (The time of the morning service was changed to 10.45am in 1887 and then, in the chapel centenary year to its present time of 11am. There is no record of the evening service being at any other time than 6pm – except during the Second World War, when it had to be brought forward into daylight hours to comply with blackout regulations.)

Unlike some dissenting chapels of the period, Whiteshill has never conducted regular Sunday afternoon worship services. However the afternoons would have been well occupied with Sabbath School; very soon having nearly 100 children and some 20 adult pupils attending each week.

Sunday services were conducted by preachers provided by the Bristol Itinerant Society. Usually the same man conducted both the morning and the evening service, which would have proved convenient as the itinerant preachers were expected to walk all the way from Bristol and then back again after they had carried out their preaching duties. The accounts show the purchase of rum and biscuits; needed to revive the preachers on arrival after their six-mile walk and to fortify them ready for the return trip at the end of the day.

Nonconformist, and particularly Independent or Congregational chapels, were generally reluctant to conduct Holy Communion unless an ordained minister was present to administer the sacraments (the bread and the wine). This might account for why, during the period the chapel was served by non-ordained itinerant preachers, who made no charge for conducting services, at regular intervals a Rev Mr Walters took the services for which he was paid 10/6d for each visit.

Rev William Thorpe, the minister of Bristol's Castle Green Independent chapel, who had been one of the preachers at the chapel opening, occupied the pulpit again for a couple of evening services, including on the chapel's first anniversary. He should have felt at home, the pulpit having been donated to Whiteshill by his church when in 1815 Castle Green chapel was re-built on a larger scale.

Rev Rowland Hill, who preached the very first sermon at the opening of the chapel, returned for a Sunday service in October 1821. The verse on which he expounded on that occasion was 2 Peter chapter 1 verse 4, *'Whereby are given unto us exceeding great and precious promises; that by these ye might be partakers of the divine nature, having escaped the corruption that is in the world through lust.'*

A careful account of expenditure and income was kept from the very beginning in a hardback foolscap book, its cover embossed with the chapel name. Produced by a renowned paper manufacturer in Cheddar and costing 10/6d, it contains over 450 pages, each one watermarked with the year of manufacture (1814) or a logo showing a seated Britannia topped by a crown.

Initially used to record important resolutions, the book contains annual accounts for every year, right through to 1966 – the 150th anniversary year of the church. The first, and a number of successive year's accounts, record the employment of one Jane Cole at the rate of £3 a year for attending to the cleaning of the chapel, plus the purchase of two brushes, a mop and a hand brush with which to complete her task.

150 years of accounts in a single book

From the income side of the 1816 accounts we can see that 18 payments of seat rent were made. In at least a couple of cases this was for whole families. Over the first two or three years the amount of seat rents paid doubled, an increased number of which covered couples or whole families. The congregation was certainly much larger than these figures might suggest, there being plenty of 'free' seats available for those who did not wish to, or could not afford to pay to reserve a particular seat.

No doubt week night meetings would have been held for prayer, worship and Bible study, and we know that some annual events soon began. An 1818 New Year meal was arranged at the White Horse (still a public house down the hill from the chapel to this day) for the Sabbath School children and for the '*Singers*' – in total it seems almost 150 people.

Two cooks were employed to produce a hearty meal of beef and mutton served with potatoes, turnips, bread and cheese, followed by fruit. All this was washed down with beer.[17]

From January 1819 the chapel was ready to release the itinerant lay preachers to other labours and call upon ordained ministers or students from theological academies to take services. For preaching Sunday morning and evening they were paid 10/6d expenses – out of which they would often choose to hire a horse, gig or coach for getting to and from the chapel.

At the same time the chapel sought to move towards running its own affairs and this brought them back to the wordy trust deed in which the basic church constitution was enshrined. The original document had given the trustees the role of appointing a minister, as long as those men and women of the congregation regularly taking Communion agreed with the choice – but the congregation wanted this the opposite way round. In other words they wanted to take the lead in selecting their own minister, and for that matter, in appointing new trustees when needed.

The trustees agreed to the change, although they were not convinced it was necessary, feeling that only a few individuals had a problem with the original wording. The alteration was put in place through the signing of a solemn pledge *'to act …. in conformity with the spirit of the proposed alterations'* as the trust deed itself could not be altered, having been legally *'Inrolled in Chancery'*.

---

[17] *This would have been low alcohol content beer, known as 'small beer', that was drunk by all ages at a time when water could well cause anything from an upset stomach to cholera.*

While at it, a couple of other matters were covered that had been accidentally left out of the conveyance when the land for the chapel was bought from Joseph Wickwick. The first was that, in line with Wickwick's wishes (remembering that he still owned the adjoining land and house), there should never be a *'burying ground'* alongside the chapel and secondly that Wickwick would have *'two sittings, free of expense'* in the chapel.

These matters settled, the deeds were deposited for safety with the deacons of Castle Green chapel in the November of 1819, to be released to the acting chapel managers, Joseph Wickwick and Nathaniel Good, if requested in writing.

Worship at Whiteshill in the early 1800s

If we were able to take ourselves back to attend a service in the early years of Whiteshill church, we might recognise the building from what we know of it today, but the 'feel' of life in the church would certainly be less familiar to us.

Serious, staid and sedate could probably sum up the style of the worship and of the congregation. Hymns would have been sung in a reverent style and at a sober pace - led by singers but with no musical accompaniment. The singers – not then called a choir - either occupied a slightly

Some of the hymn and song books used over the years.
Several years ago computer-driven screens replaced the use
of hymn books at Sunday services.

raised platform in the 'body' of the chapel or, quite likely, they sang from what we now refer to as the balcony.[18]

All the hymns would have been from those written a century earlier by the 'Father of English hymnody', Isaac Watts[19] and compiled into a book of 'Hymns and Spiritual Songs.' Of the 600 works attributed to Watts a number are still sung today, such as, 'O God, Our Help in Ages Past' and, 'When I survey the wondrous Cross'.

(In 1836, five years after it was formed, the Congregational Union published a hymn book, offering a wider selection of hymns in addition to those of Watts. Sales of this well-received volume and its later editions remained the largest source of income for the Congregational Union throughout its first few decades.)

On top of the possibility that we might sing a familiar hymn during the service, we would recognise the preaching as being very much based on exposition of the Word of God, the Bible, even though the more complex style of language

---

[18] *An item in the 1819 accounts refers to a cost for 'enclosing the singers gallery and new hatch to stairs'. As all other items in the accounts are shown individually this 'joint' entry might suggest that the section of gallery being enclosed was in what we now call the balcony – reached, as it is today, via a door to the stairs. In those days 'gallery' could mean a balcony or a low platform.*

[19] *Isaac Watts was born in 1674 and took to verse and rhyme as a very young child. A 'natural' scholar, he learnt Latin at age four, Greek at nine, French at ten and Hebrew at 13. In English nonconformist services of that time - such as in the Independent chapel of which Watts later became senior pastor - singing was almost exclusively of psalms. This 'heartless singing of psalms' frustrated Watts who felt strongly that churches should sing of Christ. Many of his hymns are based on the psalms but he added 'New Testament light' to them. His hymns gained immediate popularity despite there being a minority who objected to hymns of 'human composure'.*

used in those days would, naturally, be strange to our modern ear.

Sitting quietly waiting for the service to begin, we would find it impossible not to observe the distinction between people of different classes within the church, a reflection of early 19th Century life in general. The grooming of people's hair; their complexion – it would be clear which ones spent most days out in the fields – and their clothes; all would tell a story.

It is the Regency period but much of the fashionable attire associated with that era would have been reserved for upper class city folk and, of course for the royal Court. Nevertheless, style and quality of dress would have easily identified the social position of the various church families.

Prevailing fashion would have dictated that white was the colour to be seen in, whether it be men's breeches or ladies dresses - but only for those who could avoid walking over the muddy fields and paths to chapel. So that would have ruled out most if not all of the congregation! Yes, there were several who owned horses and carriages, but they would probably have frowned upon the use of these conveyances on the Sabbath.

While most of the women in chapel, apart from the elderly and the very poor, could be wearing similar style high-waisted 'empire line' dresses, those of the better-off ladies would have more decoration on the hem and neckline – and they would have been one of several dresses in the wardrobe from which to choose. Over their dresses, the quality and type of material from which their shawl or cape was made would also set the classes apart.

Men of some standing in the country community would be spotted by their tailored jackets – cut in to the waist with long tails and tall standing collars; a far cry from the lower class man's loose-fitting jacket – probably the only one he owned.

The working man might well be wearing a tidy, if well worn, overcoat but even this would be in contrast to the fur or velvet-collared greatcoat of his betters. For men of social standing trousers were beginning to take over from breeches, but these would still be easily distinguishable from the working man's loose, straight-legged trousers held up by a wide belt or braces.

We might notice the wealthy Walters family from Frenchay in their own area of raised seating, partitioned off from the rest of the congregation, Mr Walters having removed his quite tall, slightly conical hat upon entering the building. On the other hand, he might be someone who stuck to an older style of dress, in which case it would have been a three-cornered cocked hat he wore to chapel, but without question not a working class cap![20]

His wife, in common with all the women in the chapel would be wearing a bonnet, in her case over the top of the 'mob cap' worn at home. On a hot day, Mr and Mrs Walters could well each be carrying a wooden fan to cool them during the service, Mrs Walters having made use of a parasol to protect herself from the sun on their way to the service.

_____

[20] *The unusually flamboyant script of Walters' signature in the chapel accounts book brings to mind a man who, whatever style of clothing he adopted, would have dressed in a way that made him stand out from the crowd!*

Even within the 'floor level' pews there were specific seats reserved for those able to afford to pay six-monthly or annual seat rents. This practice dated back to the 1700s when the Independent or Congregational churches had attracted a very high proportion of *'respectable gentlemen'* whose social standing would not have made them embarrassed with the idea of paying for reserved seats in their chapel that others could not afford.

The first seating in the gallery was probably no more than simple benches – hence cheaper to rent than the ground floor pews. It would seem the early 'singers' (choir), likely to have been positioned in part of the gallery, were better accommodated.

It became the normal source of funds to meet the running costs of most Congregational churches and Whiteshill was no exception. In its first few years the annual seat rent varied between 6/- for an individual and 15/- for a family, although seats in the balcony could be less expensive.

However, the evangelical revival during which - and as a result of which - Whiteshill chapel was built, brought within its doors a much wider mix of people, for some of whom seat rents were not appropriate. So, after only three or four years additional methods of funding the church were adopted, although the letting of seats remained popular at Whiteshill throughout the 1800s and only stopped entirely in 1913.

The predominance of *'respectable gentlemen'* in the 18th Century Congregational denomination had led it – according to one prominent Congregationalist – to have become *"paralyzed by respectability and dullness"*. He went on to point out, *"It was an excellent thing that the Evangelical Revival brought into Congregationalism men and women from the farm and factory, the street and the shop: otherwise its respectability would have killed it."*

That said, by the time Whiteshill came into being, Congregational churches remained more serious, sedate and intellectual than other dissenting denominations such as the Methodists – *'the religion of excitement'*.

Humour was definitely frowned upon in church life. When a writer ventured on a little mild humour in a letter for publication in the Congregational Magazine in the 1820s, he was solemnly and ponderously rebuked by the editor who remarked: *"We consider ridicule and jest as ill-adapted to such serious subjects as those before us."*

One preacher, expressing a widely held view of the time, said that he was, *"convinced that true religion and levity are quite inconsistent with each other, and are, and ever will be, irreconcilable. Religion, if it has a prevailing influence on the mind, will be an antidote against a volatile and trifling disposition."*

One has to remember that, even in many quarters outside of the church, theatre-going and novel-reading were still taboo and other *'amusement'* discouraged as late as the 1850s. In the dissenting churches of the early 19th Century even the use of any musical instrument in worship was treated with caution.

In the case of Whiteshill, it was quite a few decades before the chapel moved beyond unaccompanied singing in its services. This could be down to the high cost of a pipe organ – for which there was no real alternative available in the first decades of the 19th Century – but it is more likely that the first worshippers preferred not to have one.

Several big Congregational churches built in the City of Bristol after Whiteshill, and backed financially by some of the same trustees, decided against installing a musical instrument despite having enough funding to do so had they wished. Mid-century, a Yorkshire church which re-opened its organ by a *'Grand Performance'* of sacred music on Easter Monday afternoon was mercilessly pilloried in the 'Christian Witness' publication.

As we sit in the pew, now knowing we will be singing the hymns 'a cappella', our minds might turn to how 'good' the sermon will be. Well, in 1816 the Independent or Congregational churches were recognised as being served by the most well educated and theologically trained ministers of any of the denominations – and proud of the fact.

On top of that, only students who could relate a personal conversion experience were accepted for training. Independency had a long record of sound training for the ministry – four, five and often six years at its academies. In 1808 it was said of the Independent churches that, *'no denomination can boast of so great a number of ministers who preach the gospel in purity. They are all men of action, and their studies are blended with the labours of the pulpit, and the care of the congregation.'*

True as this was, with the rapid growth of Independent chapels there were for a time instances of *'illiterates in the ministry'*- but none are recorded at Whiteshill! Josiah Conder, one of the foremost Congregational laymen, wrote in 1831 that such ministers were, *'a small and decreasing proportion'* and that, *'half-educated ministers, pulpit fops, beardless pedants, and rhapsodists'* were very rare.

So, as we await the sermon at 1820s Whiteshill chapel we can rest assured that the minister is well trained; the product of one of the Independency academies. In its days as a Congregational church, many Whiteshill ministers were trained at the Bristol Theological Institute or its successor, the Congregational Western College.

The Bristol Theological Institute was established in 1863 but moved from the city in 1891 when, due to financial difficulties, it amalgamated with the Western College, Plymouth, another one of the theological schools training students primarily for the Independent/Congregational church ministry. Ten years later, the Congregational Union transferred Western College to Bristol from Plymouth where, until 1969, it remained.[21]

---

[21] *Upon moving to Bristol in 1901, Western College initially occupied temporary premises, then in 1906 a magnificent purpose-built college building was opened near the top of St Michael's Hill in Cotham, opposite the Congregational Highbury chapel. The college was designed by Bristol architect, Henry Dare Bryan in the Arts and Crafts style. The college was*

Even the Bristol Itinerant Society lay preachers who filled the Whiteshill pulpit on Sunday mornings and evenings for its first couple of years were expected to have undergone a certain amount of theological training.

As well as being well-trained Gospel preachers, it was also beneficial to the chapel that a number of Whiteshill's early ministers were men of 'independent means', using their own money to generously support the chapel – while receiving only the meagre stipend that the country chapel could afford to offer.

---

closed in 1969 and its work absorbed with that of the Congregational College at Whalley Range in Manchester, later becoming Northern Congregational College and in 1984 moved to Rushholme. The Grade ll listed college building in Bristol served as the offices of the Southern Universities Joint Examination Board during the 1970s and 80s and currently houses a GP family practice serving North West Bristol.*

Start of church membership

From the middle of 1820 Rev Mr Thomas Spilsbury became an increasingly frequent visiting preacher at Whiteshill. He had not long since arrived in Bristol, having felt it necessary to leave his thriving church in Tewksbury due to suffering from *"nervous agitation"* – possibly what would now be diagnosed as epilepsy. He was soon assisting his good friend Rev Samuel Lowell, the minister of Bristol's Bridge Street Independent chapel.

Lowell and his congregation were strongly committed to the work of the Itinerant Society, the organisation that had underwritten the building of the chapel at Whiteshill, so there is little doubt that it would have been Lowell who pointed Spilsbury towards helping the new chapel find its feet.

Spilsbury facilitated the congregation in organising itself into a church with members, a few 'rules' and church officers charged with specific duties. There is evidence to suggest he might have been recognised as the minister of the church until the first paid incumbent was appointed in 1822.

It was certainly Spilsbury who chaired, and signed the minutes of a special meeting on 22nd October 1820 which marked the start of a formal membership. 19 men and women agreed to *'enter into Church Fellowship'* and to *'hereby (through the influence of the divine Spirit) engage to be the Lords and to walk worthy of that vocation.'*

These first church members agreed the following resolutions:

1 That the ordinance of the Lords supper be administered every two months.
2 That a church meeting be called once every month.
3 Any person proposing him or herself shall converse with the minister and then be admitted by the church.
4 That Nathl Good be appointed to provide the Elements necefsary and take charge of the money collected paying out of it for the bread & wine the remainder to be distributed to the Poor.

Among the list of 19 names[22] are those of Nathaniel Good and his wife Hester. Successive generations kept this local family name in the members' register for over 120 years. Two family names on the list are still to be seen in Hambrook 200 years later – Simmonds and Pendock. Travelling from church towards the Ring Road you pass 'Simmonds Yard' on your right – now housing a series of small business units – and further along on the left is 'T B & H Pendock' the funeral directors. The strong Pendock family connection with Whiteshill chapel continued through into the 1980s.

On that very first members' list is the name of William Bain Addis, who went on to be the first Whiteshill member to serve overseas as a missionary. He lived with his widowed mother Elizabeth in Hambrook, before leaving in 1823 to attend Hoxton missionary college in London for several years' study.

From there he went to India on behalf of the London Missionary Society and after further 'in-country' training, was ordained in 1828. The following year Addis was sent,

---

[22] *The names include nine men, nine women and one surname without any Christian name in front of it – so whether the majority of the first members were men or were women is not known!*

with his family, to Coimbatore (in Tamal Nadu, the most southern Indian State).

He was the first Protestant missionary in the province and stayed until in 1861 ill-health forced him to retire. He spent his final ten years in Coonoor, a hill station in the same State. William, his wife Susanna and missionary son Charles are all buried in Coonoor.

Willam Bain Addis in later life in India (left) and at about the age he would have been when at Whiteshill

In Tamal Nadu William Addis is still honoured, and a road named after him, for setting up the first school for Dalits (formerly known as Untouchables) and for his work which grew into *'the cornerstone of the Coimbatore diocese of the Church of South India'*.

First resident minister

When in 1822 the Whiteshill membership felt led to 'call' Samuel Weston to be their first resident minister the result was a mad scramble to put the chapel finances on a better footing, so that he could be paid!

He was chosen from a number of students, of various theological academies, who had been invited to conduct services on several occasions. Weston completed several years study at Newtown Academy in Montgomeryshire, one of two academies in Wales for those intending to become Independent ministers. It was agreed that the 27-year-old should *'take charge of the pulpit'* every week from 10th November 1822.

As his time to start came close, it was realised that simply paying the usual 10/6d for taking the two Sunday services each week would not add up to a sufficient salary - but it was all that the finances could bear. This was despite rent from letting upward of 40 seats, collections taken up after morning and evening services on the second Sunday of each month (instigated in June 1821) plus a couple of generous annual subscriptions from wealthy donors.

There had been a Communion collection since November 1820 but that was for purchasing the bread and wine, the remainder being committed entirely to poor relief in the local community.

In fact, since the beginning, chapel treasurer (and one of two chapel managers) Nathaniel Good had been personally owed money at the end of each year when the accounts were drawn up. This was not helped by a £29/12/10 bill having been received for painting the inside and outside of the building in the previous year - the chapel having been closed for two Sundays in May 1821 during the redecorating.

So, as a short term measure, trustee John Godwin and three of the founding church members Joseph King, Nathaniel Good and Jonathan Pendock each made one-off contributions enabling Weston's salary to be supplemented for the remainder of 1822.

At an 'eleventh hour' meeting in the vestry, 12 members and friends decided to pay 6d (in most cases), each and every week, beyond what they were already giving, *'towards Liquidating the Debt which is now due to Nathl Good from this Chapel and Also for increasing the salary of a resident Minister'*. This giving continued for several years, although latterly being collected on a quarterly basis.

The chapel now felt able to provide a salary of £12/10/0 per quarter to Weston. Over two or three years the finances moved from a deficit into a small surplus, even if to achieve this meant a handful of better-off members each making a special donation at the year's end to ensure the books balanced.

Weston's £50 annual salary was not high but none the less not untypical for a country chapel minister. A few big city churches were able to offer high salaries of £300, or even in extremely rare cases up to £700 a year, but on the other hand it was quite usual for rural ministers to have to exist on £40 or as little as £30 a year. Many ministers had 'private means' with which to supplement their salary, as did several of the Whiteshill incumbents through into the opening decades of the 20th Century.

Independent or Congregational ministers were renowned for being 'learned' and the four to six years full-time study at a theological academy to attain this standard of training and education naturally worked in favour of those from wealthy families who could afford to fund their son through these 'non-earning' years.

Little can be gleaned about Weston's ministry – nor for that matter for the following few ministers – as almost the only records we have to go on for that period are the annual accounts of *'receivings and disbursements'* [income and expenditure]. These show monthly offerings and subscriptions staying steady during Weston's years at Whiteshill, but a doubling of seat rents, suggesting a healthy increase in the numbers attending services.

There was no drop-off in the amount collected at each *'sacrament'* [Communion] service when these were doubled in frequency, being conducted on the first Sunday of every month from mid-1823.

The drive within any Independent chapel at the time was very much focussed on taking its witness to Christ beyond the doors of the church to the wider community and to instructing the local children through Sabbath (or Sunday) School. There can be no doubt that these would have been priorities for the Whiteshill minister.

Weston was *'ordained to the pastoral office at White's-hill'* in June of the year after he arrived. The first of the day's two services was introduced by Rev Thomas Spilsbury, who had played a major role in guiding the congregation before they 'called' their first full-time paid minister. Rev Samuel Lowell (Bridge Street chapel) and Rev William Thorpe (Castle Green chapel), ministers at the forefront of the work of the Itinerant Society that was behind the creation of the chapel, also took part.

The record of Whiteshill infant baptisms by '*Minister of the Gospel Samuel Weston*' gives a feel for the way Independent churches were reaching out beyond what had become the denomination's traditional upper-class adherents. Those baptised encompassed sons and daughters of labourers and tool-grinders through to a school master and well-to-do farm owners.

As an aside, among the record of those baptised by Weston are the baby daughter and then a son of Robert and Sarah (nee Walters) Simmonds – two of the original (but at that time unmarried) chapel members. The fact that the Walters' status merited their own partitioned-off raised seating area in the chapel had obviously not stopped Robert wooing Sarah and them getting married.

Once wed, I am sure the strict social etiquette of that time would have dictated whether Robert was 'elevated' into the Walters' '*gallery*' for Sunday services or whether Sarah was demoted to Robert's rented pew in the main body of the chapel!

In Spring 1828 it was Weston's turn to get married; to Mary Brodribb, a farmer's daughter of Clutton, Somerset. The Brodribbs[23] were one of two prosperous families who had been mainstays of Clutton Independent chapel since it was built in 1813, on leasehold land held by the family. But the wedding ceremony had to take place at the Anglican parish church.

_____

[23] *Famous Victorian actor-manager Sir Henry Irving was a member of the Brodribb family of Clutton; Irving was only a stage name. He was born John Henry Brodribb in 1838, first took to the stage in 1856, became manager of the Lyceum Theatre in 1878 and was knighted in 1895 – the first knighthood ever bestowed upon an actor.*

No doubt the young couple would have much preferred to make their vows in the Independent chapel which Mary attended, but the law prohibiting weddings being performed at dissenting chapels was not changed until the best part of another decade.

The social class of Mary's father entitled him to use the title 'Esquire' after his name and Weston himself came from a Shropshire family of equal standing.

The Weston's first child, Thomas[24], was born towards the end of 1829 and baptised - at Whiteshill - the following February, by Rev. Evan James who had attended the same academy as Weston and was by then minister of the Welsh-speaking Independent chapel in Bristol's Lower Castle Street. The errors, omissions and corrections in Weston's hand-written 'log' of baptisms might suggest that his talents lay in other directions than record-keeping.

---

[24] *Weston's son, Thomas, who had been born at Whiteshill, went on to become a doctor, practising as a GP in London.*

Ministers and home missionaries

For eight years Whiteshill's first full-time minister, Samuel Weston, was paid his salary on the due day each quarter without fail, but behind the scenes finance was becoming an issue again by the close of the 1820s. Two wealthy members who were probably providing a good proportion of the chapel's income had died – Nathaniel Good in January 1829 and Howell Walters in 1830. This led to the chapel only being able to pay Weston less than half his salary in 1831.

The only answer was for Weston to move on, which he did in March 1832. Three cash advances were provided to ensure that the outstanding salary was paid to Weston before his departure – the loans soon being repaid once the burden of a minister's salary had been lifted. Weston moved with his young family to become *'Protestant Dissenting Minister of Wooham, Bucks'*, where he continued for the next quarter of a century.

Once during each month until a new minister was in place, a horse or *'conveyance'* was hired, more than likely to transport an ordained minister to Whiteshill to take Sunday services and in particular to conduct Communion. Other Sundays, local lay preachers would have led services and preached. The record of church *'disbursements'* [expenses] lists payment for several letters, arriving from various localities[25], possibly to do with 'booking' Sunday speakers and one or two definitely to do with appointing a new minister.

Most intriguingly, there are expenses during this time referring to two court cases; the chapel paying the Hambrook Constable, Thomas Gay, to serve summonses on a number of local individuals, followed by the church caretaker/sexton and a couple of other members attending the 'Justices' Meeting' to appear as witnesses.

The entries in the accounts give no clue as to the nature – nor the outcome - of the court proceedings. One of the few other expenses listed at this time is for a padlock, to be fitted on the coal house door, so could it be that the accused had been spotted helping themselves to the chapel fuel?

Something else it would be interesting to know more about happened in February 1833. In that month, the chapel registered with the office of the Bishop of Bristol a 'certificate' required by law when a dissenting chapel was being formed. This is strange as the chapel had been in existence for 16 years by now, and a 'certificate' had already been lodged with the office of the Bishop of Gloucester when the church was founded in 1816.

---

[25] *Until the country-wide introduction of the 'Penny Post' in 1840 (by postal reformer Rowland Hill who is said to have been given his Christian name in admiration of famous preacher Rev Rowland Hill, the preacher at the opening of Whiteshill chapel) delivery of letters was paid for by the recipient. The cost depended on the distance the letter had travelled and the number of pages – envelopes being rarely used as they counted as a further page. The amounts charged were prohibitively high; the chapel paid 1/- for one letter and 6d or 7d for others. Even one from very nearby cost 4d.*

In mid-November 1833, a new man, Mr W Ellson [he is the one minister whose first name is not known] had taken board and lodgings in the village and was embarking upon his ministry at Whiteshill. He was partly funded through a grant from the Home Missionary Society, supplemented by an annual £35 salary from the chapel, paid in quarterly amounts.

The Home Mission Society had been founded in 1819 to promote evangelistic preaching and Sunday Schools in town and country. It began as an *'undenominational'* work but soon became identified solely with the Independent or Congregational denomination.

Ellson, one of about 30 home missionaries at the time, was ordained in August 1834 at Whiteshill – *'a place of worship'* which had, according to the report in the Evangelical Magazine and Missionary Chronicle, *'become the centre of an important station, being surrounded by many populous villages, affording a wide field for missionary labours.'* Giving the 'charge' to the new incumbent at the ordination services was Rev W Henry of Tooting, the secretary to the Mission.

A cleric of the day who helped churches find suitable ministers had the view that, *'Independent ministers were well educated, but the Home Missionary Society had brought many uneducated but earnest men into its service'*. We know nothing of Ellson's training but it is interesting to note that in the financial accounts, unlike other Whiteshill ministers, he is referred to throughout as *'Mr Ellson'*; never *'Rev Ellson'*.

This time there was no financial problem, but nevertheless in October 1835, barely two years after arriving, Ellson moved on to *'labour'* at another Home Mission *'station'* possibly at Pill in Somerset. He did return to preach at the services on the final Sunday of the year.

Ellson's departure was followed by a longer gap, of four years, during which time Edmund H Duval[26] from Bristol agreed to be responsible for *'supplying the pulpit'* with preachers, who were paid 5/- for conducting the two Sunday services. During this period there were just two church deacons; recorded as *'Mssrs Perry and Simmons'* - Thomas Perry [27] and the chapel treasurer William Simmonds (sometimes spelt with a 'd' and other times without – made more confusing by there being two prominent chapel families with the same surname!), who were signing off the annual accounts.

The next minister, Rev John Averill, arrived with his family[28] in the latter part of 1839. His name is also spelt as Avaril, Avarhill or Averhill in various church records! Once again his salary was supplemented by the Home Mission Society and the church was now in a position,

---

[26] *Duval was headmaster of a large British school in Bristol until 1845, after which he emigrated to Canada, having been invited to set up a British Model school in New Brunswick. He went on to become Chief Inspector of Schools for the City and County of St John in New Brunswick.*

[27] *Born in Cambridgeshire about 1797, Thomas Perry lived in Hambrook for around 20 years from the late 1820s, building up a business as a 'wool stapler'- separating wool out into different grades for selling on to manufacturers. By 1851 he had moved to Winchester, leaving behind the eldest of his nine children, William, also a wool stapler.*

[28] *Averill's family consisted of two Carolines! His wife Caroline (nee Beard) whom he had married in summer 1832 and their only child Caroline Beard Averill who was born a little over a year later, so would have been coming up to her sixth birthday when the family moved to Whiteshill. Daughter Caroline lived with her parents throughout their lives, as an adult 'living on her own means' with the assistance of the one, then two, live-in servants employed by the family in later years.*

having grown in size, to pay Averill £10 a quarter, topped up in some years by a further £5 or £10 payment.

In an unusual arrangement, any financial surplus in hand at the end of the year was also given to Averill. The congregation obviously thought he was well worth his money, as, in the one year when there was next-to-no surplus, members contributed generously so that he did not have to forgo his 'year-end bonus'.

In 1843 the Home Mission was having to reduce the subscription given to its missionaries as the Society's attempt to fund the growing work through asking churches to give a penny a week only gained the support of some 300 of the more than 2000 Congregational churches. When the Whiteshill congregation found that Averill's subscription had been reduced from £40 to £30 a year they had a special collection, raising several pounds of the difference.

In his early thirties when he came to Whiteshill, Averill stayed for five and a half years before moving on to a church at Moreton-in-Marsh. Although originally from Staffordshire he spent his ministerial life mostly in the West of England and of the nine or ten different churches of which he was pastor, Whiteshill was his longest stay.

He seems to have been much liked at Whiteshill and at other churches of which he was pastor over 35 years of ministry, but Averill was not always immune from controversy. He had originally been ordained as a Wesleyan Methodist minister, in 1832, upon completion of that denomination's normal four year probationary period and was appointed minister of a Wesleyan chapel in Teignmouth.

In 1835 he was 'stationed' in the Camelford circuit but was soon suspended for siding with the majority of the congregation instead of supporting the decisions of the local Superintendent. Expulsion as a Methodist minister followed a full hearing in front of the Wesleyan Conference and led him to join the Independents.

He was the subject of a widely-circulated anti-dissenter pamphlet some 15 years later. It criticised the fact that individual dissenting congregations, unlike those of the established church, chose and paid their own ministers.

To illustrate what the writer saw as the shortcomings of the practice, it cited at length Averills' strong words after being *'compelled to resign his pastorate'* at Kingsbridge Independent Chapel after only eight months *'in consequence of a rupture in his congregation'* when his *'views were not hyper-Calvanistic enough to satisfy some of the carping critics'*.

His final spell as a pastor was a short time at Bradford on Avon from 1865 to 1866, although he had already all-but retired from the ministry due to *'severe ill-health'*, that had ended a three-year ministry at Christchurch Chapel in Clevedon – where he had a purse of 100 guineas [£105] presented to him on relinquishing his duties.

Back with the Itinerant Society

Whiteshill minister Rev John Averill left in 1845, around the time in May of what was beginning to be an annual event - the church anniversary tea; tickets for which raised a good sum for chapel funds.

It being not yet three decades since the chapel was built, lots of the congregation must have been aware that the church opened in August, not May, but maybe they reckoned the weather was better for an outdoor tea in May, or possibly many would have been too busy with the harvest in August to organise or attend an anniversary tea.

The tea would be followed by a *'public meeting'* (a service with a visiting preacher) and handbills were printed and delivered to local houses by caretaker/sexton William Reed or, from 1850, William Pritchard, to advertise these events. Some years later, for a period of time, the date of anniversary tea and meetings came much nearer to the correct time of the year, moving to mid-October.

After Averill's departure, it was to be another 20 years before Whiteshill 'called' another resident minister, but in the meanwhile there was plenty of activity. In particular, like many churches, attention turned to finding ways of running a school, beyond the Sunday Schools that by now few churches were without.

There were night schools in operation at Whiteshill by 1845 but the Sunday School teachers and others started a day school in 1849, teaching some 30 to 40 youngsters. Having only the chapel itself and a very small vestry in which to meet probably made this a fairly difficult undertaking and it was discontinued several years later.

Church income dipped in these years, not because of any decrease in church numbers, but more likely, with no minister to pay, members diverted what they could afford to give into the fund for running a day school and later for building the school rooms to the back of the chapel.

The church had been arranging and paying ministers to conduct services since it had been without a resident pastor but from the beginning of 1848 it was decided the church would come back under the wing of the Bristol Itinerant Society as far as providing preachers Sunday by Sunday was concerned.

The arrangement was that the church made an annual donation, usually £5, and the Society provided the preachers as they had when the church was first founded – but by now the itinerant preachers were no longer expected to walk to where they were conducting services.

From 1847 the Itinerant Society had begun to allow claims from preachers for *'conveyances'* and paid £10 towards the cost of two new *'coburgs'* (carriages). In 1858 the Whiteshill accounts show the purchase of *'Cobourg Cloth and Fringe'* which could have been to produce a covering for an open carriage, to make life more comfortable for the travelling preachers.

But that can only be a guess as the cloth could have been for some other use inside the chapel. In 1876 two new coburgs, with four wheels, were built specially for the Society, but that was after Whiteshill once again had its own minister.

It had become legal from 1836 for ministers of nonconformist churches to conduct wedding ceremonies but church record books that would show if any took place at Whiteshill do not go back far enough. Equally, no record has been found of infant baptisms until after this period of the church's history, apart from the 'log' kept by the very first minister covering babies he baptised between 1824 and 1832. If any weddings or baptisms did take place at the chapel it would be interesting to know who conducted them – presumably a 'visiting' ordained minister.

In the 1851 Religious Census[29] Whiteshill deacon Moses Young[30], reported a morning congregation of 70 adults plus 40 Sunday School children; 70 children at afternoon Sunday School and 180 adults at the evening service. The census return stated that the chapel had seating for 360 people, of which 140 seats were rented or available to rent.

With the founding of the chapel 40 years distant, in 1856 it was necessary to look at appointing new chapel trustees as only five of the original 13 were able to continue, most of the others having died by then. It was an opportunity to include, for the first time, some of the church members to serve alongside trustees from the Bristol Itinerant Society.

---

[29] *Alongside the ten-yearly population census of 1851 the government carried out a controversial census on Accommodation and Attendance at Worship, generally referred to as a Religious Census. All places of worship were required to make a return giving a specified breakdown of seating capacity and attendance for Sunday 30th March. The results, indicating that 'only' 50 to 60% of 'eligible attendees' had gone to church that day, were seen in mid-19th Century as an indictment of the ungodly state into which the country had descended.*

[30] *In 1851 Moses Young, a 37-years-old master currier, lived in Hambrook with his wife, Eliza, and their eight children, two of whom were his apprentices. He also employed three men on 11 acres of local land. A currier was a specialist in the leather processing industry. After the tanning process, the currier applies techniques of dressing, finishing and colouring to the tanned hide to make it strong, flexible and waterproof.*

At a vestry meeting chaired by Arley Chapel minister Rev Samuel Hebditch[31], two names well-known to this day were among the new chapel trustees appointed: H O Wills (probably H O Wills ll) and Handel Cossham[32]. They were listed, respectively, on the revised Trust document simply as, *'Tobacconist'* and *'Coal Merchant'*.

Trustees appointed from the chapel membership were Moses Young (*Currier*), William Simmons (*Hatter*), Howell Simmonds (*Painter*) and Thomas Edwards (*Shoemaker*).

Itinerant Society treasurer John Godwin, who had personally contributed a large proportion of the building costs back in the 1810s remained as a trustee, with two of his sons and his son-in-law joining him as trustees. John Godwin continued to contribute generously to the running costs of the church until his death less than two years later.

School rooms were built onto the back of the chapel in about 1860 for what then became the home of the Whiteshill British Day School for the next half a century. With the money having been found to erect these rooms and the day school getting well established, the congregation began to

---

[31] *Rev Samuel Hebditch was the minister of Arley Chapel, Cheltenham Road, Bristol (now the Polish Roman Catholic church) for 17 years. After a time at a London church, in 1880 he embarked for Australia to pastor a church in Melbourne for a year, partly on account of his son's poor health. The steamship SORATA, on which the family were travelling, ran aground and was wrecked off Adelaide but all the passengers were rescued. Hebditch never returned to England and later became chairman of the Congregational Union in Australia.*

[32] *Handel Cossham, a Congregational lay-preacher born in Thornbury, had in 1851 opened Parkfield Colliery at Pucklechurch and went on to open other collieries locally. He was Mayor of Bath from 1882 and Bristol East MP from 1885. Cossham Hospital in Kingswood is a memorial to Handel Cossham, who instructed in his will that his estate be used for the building of a hospital.*

think about the feasibility of having a resident minister once again.

A *'Ministers Fund'* was set up and individuals sought who would commit to donate a set amount to the fund each quarter towards a minister's salary. The good amount pledged gave the church confidence to embark upon seeking another full-time minister after two decades without one.

A day school for the local children

It is the 1860s. School mistress Elizabeth Dennis is keeping a close eye on up to 80 boys and girls, aged from three to 13 years old, from her vantage point on the raised platform at

the front of the room. This crowded 40 by 21 feet [12m by 6.4m] schoolroom behind the chapel is home to the Whiteshill Day School. Dennis has previously been instructing the whole school from the platform – known as gallery teaching – and now the pupils are spread around the room in 'drafts' or groups of about ten.

In the centre of the room, sitting on benches (backs to which, let alone desks, not arriving in any numbers until 1889 onwards) are a draft practicing their writing skills on individual slates.

The route to school for the poor working class children of the village from 1860

Each of the other groups of pupils is standing - as they did for most of the school day - receiving instruction and reciting facts using charts fixed on the wall at various points round the edge of the room.

Each group is being taught by a monitor - a bright pupil of maybe only ten or 11 years old who might be paid around a penny a week to supervise other children while hopefully furthering his or her own education with instruction from Mistress Dennis at lunch time, or for an hour before or after school.

This picture of school life at Whiteshill, under what was known as the *'Monitorial'* system, would have been closely mirrored at church schools across the country. For the children of almost every 'ordinary' family this was the only educational opportunity available, and then only if their parents could afford fees which, at Whiteshill, were two pence a week per child in 1869; although later lowered a little under competition from other church schools in the locality.

In many respects, these schools were a natural extension to the work of the Sunday Schools that flourished from their beginnings in the 1780s. The Sunday School movement's purpose was to teach children to be able to read the Bible and in the words of Christian educational pioneer, Hannah More, *'to train up the lower classes in habits of industry and piety'*.

At the time, even amongst those, like Moore, who approved of teaching the poor and working classes to read – and many did not – there was a widely held view that mastering writing was an unnecessary accomplishment for such children.

But changes taking place in British society fuelled a desire for a fuller education to be made available to all. While radical thinkers were open to government, for the first time, getting involved in the provision of education for the country's infants, the Church of England saw itself as the rightful guardian of spiritual – and that included educational – matters.

The nonconformist churches, such as the Congregationalists with which Whiteshill was aligned, also saw education as fundamentally a religious issue in which the State had no part to play. Equally, they were anxious that education should not be left solely in the hands of the established church. By the 1840s the Congregational Union was encouraging all its churches, wherever possible, to start day schools.

However, at the same time the Union, along with the Baptists, was totally opposed to accepting government grants which had become available from 1833 towards the costs of building and running such schools. By the mid-1840s the Congregational Union had raised over £120,000 in donations and subscriptions to be used to build its own schools, thus avoiding the need to accept any state aid, which they saw as government interference endangering the religious nature of education.

Whiteshill chapel, of course, had a strong commitment to Sabbath or Sunday School from its very beginnings and it is recorded that as well as going on to organise adult evening classes, in 1849 its Sunday School teachers and others organised - for exactly how long is not said – day-schooling for about 30 to 40 local children.

Whether or not the chapel applied for funding from the Congregational Union school-building 'pot' is unknown, but if it did seek financial help it was obviously not one of the several hundred successful bids, as the Whiteshill school did not gain a dedicated school room at this time.

Lack of funding might account for why this first attempt to run a day school at the chapel could not be sustained. It would have proved difficult in a rural area to raise sufficient subscriptions to survive in the absence of government or Congregational Union funding. In any case, without the benefit of a purpose-built school room, operating a school would have been tricky using only a church full of pews.

Whiteshill's two school rooms, built onto the back of the church in two storeys, did not materialise until a decade later, funded this time with the help of a grant in the year 1861 from the British & Foreign Schools Society. (Schools associated with this society were known as 'British' schools.) The addition of these state-of-the-art (for those days!) facilities resulted in the growth of a successful and long-lasting week-day school offering a very creditable standard of elementary education to children of the local labouring or poor classes.

Some of about 150 children aged between three and 14 years old who were pupils at the Whiteshill day school in 1893, pictured with the headmaster and the infants' teacher.

As a 'British' school Whiteshill employed the '*Monitorial*' system – using monitors for the bulk of the teaching. This method of delivering elementary schooling to children of the working classes, had been developed as an efficient, scientific – and cheap - approach to mass education by Quaker, Joseph Lancaster, in the first decade of the 19th Century.

Most nonconformist church schools were 'British' schools and so applied the highly detailed educational methods built by Lancaster around his concept. The training of early British school teachers was primarily in mastering the intricacies of Lancaster's teaching system.

Church of England clergyman, Dr Andrew Bell, designed a very similar teaching system, which was used in the far more numerous 'National' schools of the Church of England. Bell and Lancaster's invention of the *'Monitorial'* system was hailed as *'a piece of social machinery that was both simple and economical'*.

Elementary education of the nation's lower class children being centred on Christian teaching and principles was inherent in the operation of both the British and the National schools. Equally, this was accepted by successive governments as, over time, they became involved in part-funding and inspecting more and more church schools. As one government-appointed school inspector stated in the 1840s, *"The 'classics' of the poor in a Protestant country must ever, indeed, be the Scriptures: they contain the most useful of all knowledge."*

The stated aim of the British schools was to discipline *'the infant poor to good and orderly habits, to train them in early piety'*. A typical expression of the purpose of a National school was, *'to confer upon the children of the poor the inestimable benefit of religious instruction, combined with such other acquirements as may be suitable to their stations in life ...'*

The full titles of the National and of the British school societies give a similar insight not only into the relationship between education and religion in the mid-19th Century but also underline the strong class structure prevailing in that era. Their complete names were, *The National Society for Promoting the Education of the Poor in the Principles of the Established Church*, and, *The British and Foreign School Society for the Education of the Labouring and Manufacturing Classes of Society of every Religious Persuasion.*

There was little expectation, or wish amongst much of the establishment, that pupils of these schools would go on beyond elementary education. The Whiteshill day school log shows only three or four pupils moving on to a secondary school – two of whom were the daughters of the school's headmaster from 1885, Levi Luff. Constance Dora and then Edith Marion Luff each won scholarships, by examina⋅⋅on, to Colston Girls school in the opening years of the 20th Century.

The Whiteshill school records and accounts were kept entirely separate from those of the church itself but the congregation, including prominent church members such as local gentleman (and chapel treasurer) Jacob Dove, were behind much of its funding and the church kept a close eye on its progress throughout the 50 years of its existence.

Successive ministers of the chapel over that half century were automatically chairman of the school governors and, as they were required to, paid regular visits, in particular to verify the attendance records. Other members of the management committee – most, if not all, from the chapel - inspected the school from time to time. Their wives in some cases not only visited but supervised groups of girls in knitting and sewing; considered a vital part of the curriculum.

One man in particular who devoted much time and effort to setting up, supporting and managing the school, was

Hambrook wool-stapler and farmer William Perry [33] (the eldest son of 1840s chapel deacon Thomas Perry). Upon Perry's death in November 1900, the pupils were given the afternoon off, allowing their headmaster to attend the funeral of *'one of the founders of this school and who has always continued to show a great interest in its welfare'*.

---

[33] *Born in 1821, William Perry lived by, and ran, the Wool Warehouse in Hambrook where as a wool-stapler he bought in wool from producers for his employees to sort and grade before selling it on to woollen manufacturers. He also farmed 30 acres of local land. Whiteshill chapel having no burial ground, Perry was buried at the Unitarian chapel in Frenchay.*

Changes in educational thinking

One mistress, or master, keeping 80 or more three to 13 year-olds in order in the two-room day school behind Whiteshill chapel – let alone teaching them to read, write, do sums and importantly, conducting scripture lessons - would be a tall order today, and no less so in the second half of the 1800s.

The use of young monitors teaching small groups was seen as the *'efficient and scientific'* answer to making this system of schooling work, but to stop things ending up in chaos and confusion, the British and Foreign Schools Society, whose teaching methods were followed by Whiteshill day school, created very detailed organisational rules.

The Society's 1831 *Manual of the System of Primary Instruction* listed verbal commands and alternative hand signals for everything that would happen during the school day. A school's mistress or master would pass this code on to the monitors, who would then ensure the pupils knew what to do upon hearing – or seeing – the commands given. The manual even included sequences of drawings showing precisely how pupils had to respond to the commands!

All the indications are that Whiteshill day school adhered to the manual from when the school rooms first opened in the early 1860s. Schoolmistress Elizabeth Dennis, in 1869, was supported by only one monitor, although she might well have used other pupils as unofficial, unpaid monitors. But into the following decade, there were changes in educational thinking, in part to deal with the by then generally recognised shortcomings of using only untrained young monitors in support of a solitary teacher.

In a drive to improve teaching standards, schools were being encouraged to move away from the *'Monitorial'* pattern of teaching by replacing untrained monitors with 'apprentices' known as Pupil Teachers. For a time, there were Education Department financial incentives for schools to employ pupil teachers, who were required to be at least 13 years of age, undertook extra learning in their own time over the course of five years and had to pass an annual examination.

In the case of Whiteshill, monitors, who in later years were expected to be a little older and to have at least a certain amount of education beyond that of other pupils, continued to be used right up to the school's closure, alongside one or two pupil teachers. Not every pupil teacher turned out to be as beneficial as expected! Maria Baylis, accepted as the pupil teacher in 1871, was by the end of the year being *'reproved for neglecting her homework'*.

After that she appeared to make steady progress and pass the required exam year-by-year until in her fifth, and final, probationary year she did very badly in composition, geography and history – *'her papers in these subjects are most discreditable'*. Needless to say, shortly afterwards, *'Miss Baylis completed her engagement as PT'* as the school log politely phrased her departure.

The next pupil teacher, Harry Symonds, did even worse. He only lasted for about three years before being sacked. Successive masters frequently *'admonished'* and *'cautioned'* him for being too familiar with the pupils, fighting with pupils outside the school, being late, being careless in lesson preparation, quarrelling, telling falsehoods and timewasting!

It became *'out of the question to have him as Pupil Teacher'* when, as the master reported, *'Symonds, I found actually playing a game of chance with one of the boys in the class. He was playing what is generally called Heads or Tails with a halfpenny … I have so many times warned him about his behaviour that this time I sent him home and decided to bring the matter before the Managers.'*

Entries in the Whiteshill school daily log begin in 1870, leading to the conclusion that this was the point the school managers started accepting government grants. The Congregational Union had, a couple of years earlier, realised they had to go along with the principle of state financial help after more than a quarter of a century of opposition.

Individual Congregational churches had never been bound by the Union stance of not accepting state aid for their schools and many had long before started taking funding from the government. Whiteshill seems to have kept in line with the Congregational Union opposition to state aid for schools until the Union's national annual conference reversed its no-grant policy.

Conditions placed on schools that received government funds included, among other things, keeping a daily log of school activity and submitting to an annual inspection. Before a school could be considered for any grant money it had to be employing a *'certificated'* (college qualified) mistress or master. This requirement could account for the change of Whiteshill's school mistress at the beginning of 1870.

Elizabeth Dennis had been the school mistress during the 1860s. She had completed five years as a pupil teacher as a teenager in the 1850s at a school in her native Devonport but at the end of this she had not gained a *'Queen's Scholarship'*. This scholarship would have allowed her to attend a teacher training college for two years to become a certificated teacher.

Without this qualification she could not be in charge of a school receiving government grants. With most schools now relying on such funding, Dennis had little option but to change career entirely. Moving back to Devon she became a grocer in West Teignmouth.

The school managers were no doubt relieved to have access to government grants, even if they still harboured doubts about the acceptability of government inspections being made of a church school. However, as grants were not permitted to total more than 50% of a school's costs, the church still had to secure local backers and find other ways to raise funds to meet its share of each year's running expenses.

Despite individuals in the church pledging subscriptions to fund the school, it struggled at times to make ends meet. During at least one winter no coal could be afforded to heat the school room. Performances by the church choir and singing by the pupils themselves were used to raise funds. In one particular year the church 'abandoned the Xmas Tree Bazaar' so the school could hold its own Christmas fundraiser, after the school committee appealed for £20, having found themselves in serious debt.

For most of the years the school existed, government grants were awarded on the basis of the average number of children aged over six years old in attendance, hence the insistence on an accurate register. On top of this grant, through into the 1890s a payment was earned by the school for each child who satisfied the school inspector in tests at six different '*standards*' (or levels) of reading, writing, arithmetic and later in other approved subjects such as history and geography.

Those under six years-of-age were exempt from these tests and a grant awarded subject to a general report by the inspector as to the suitability of their education. The inspector, on most occasions, found the older Whiteshill children well taught, saying for instance in 1872, '*The children read with an amount of intelligence which is remarkable in a country school*'. Early on, they were less satisfied with the teaching of the very youngest children to the point that the full grant for the 'under-sixes' was refused after inspections in 1876 and 1877.

The inspector had found the 'under-sixes' were not being looked after by a pupil teacher, nor even a monitor, but by one of the older girl pupils – and what he seemingly found the most unsatisfactory, it was a different girl each week. His strong recommendation was the appointment of a paid monitor and in fact two more were appointed, one specifically for the infants.

In many schools, Whiteshill included, new educational ideas had an influence on how the 'under-sixes' - the infants - were taught. A more informal approach was adopted with this age group during the 1860s, including the use of music, toys and other equipment – and most of all a new level of kindness! At Whiteshill, a section at the back of the schoolroom was partitioned off especially for the infants.

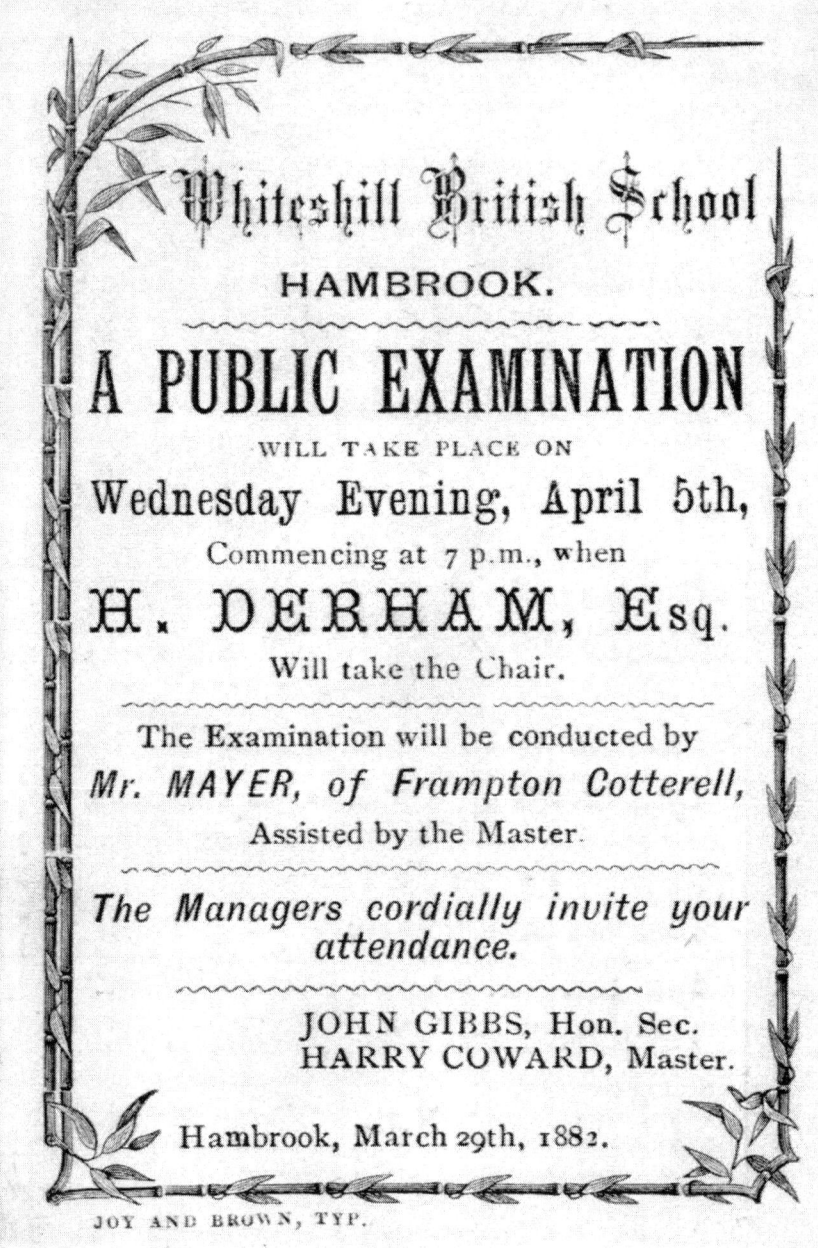

Whiteshill British School

HAMBROOK.

A PUBLIC EXAMINATION

WILL TAKE PLACE ON

Wednesday Evening, April 5th,

Commencing at 7 p.m., when

H. DERHAM, Esq.

Will take the Chair.

The Examination will be conducted by

Mr. MAYER, of Frampton Cotterell,

Assisted by the Master.

The Managers cordially invite your attendance.

JOHN GIBBS, Hon. Sec.
HARRY COWARD, Master.

Hambrook, March 29th, 1882.

JOY AND BROWN, TYP.

*It really was a **public** examination! Between the children singing and reciting poems they were tested in Mental Arithmetic, Reading, Grammar and Manual Exercises*

It is said that the infants learnt to trace out the letters of the alphabet in trays of sand and even if they later had slates, it took until 1902 to introduce the use of paper and lead pencils to the youngest children. *'Slate work'* was a regular part of the school day for most of the age groups for many years – with the school inspector in 1885 calling for sponges to be provided as he observed that, *'the manner in which the slates are cleaned is objectionable.'* He was obviously not a 'spit and polish' man!

This 1894 photograph appears to show the under-sixes, about one-third of the school - with their teacher Martha Pendock (left).

Object Lessons, a new and soon popular educational idea, came in as a strong feature of learning both with the infants and with the older children, only gradually going out of fashion in the first decade of the 20th Century.

Progression from the original British School teaching system went further with the employment of an infants' teacher – first, for a brief period of time, Miss Edwards[34] then from 1878 Miss Martha Pendock. A couple of years later, initially as an experiment, the infants moved into the upstairs room which, until then, does not appear to have been used by the school in the 20 years since the two school rooms had been built, apart from for girls' sewing lessons.

There was a concern that being upstairs would put the infants *rather too much removed from the Masters' superintendence* but with changing attitudes to teaching these youngest pupils, a dedicated infants' teacher now being on the staff, plus the total size of the school having grown to close on 100 children, it became a permanent feature of the school – as did Martha Pendock. She remained the infants' teacher right through to the school being replaced in 1911 by the newly-built Council school on the other side of Whiteshill Common.

---

[34] *This appears to have been teenager Amelia Edwards, youngest daughter of Whiteshill chapel trustee and senior deacon, Thomas Edwards. Amelia went on to become a certificated school mistress, teaching at a school in Sussex before giving up her career upon marrying at the close of the 1800s.*

Day school outgrows its premises

Looking back at the surviving Whiteshill church school log covering the 40 years up to its closure in 1911, it seems amazing that the school succeeded in providing the good elementary education that school inspectors found it did.

Of course, by its nature the daily log – a strict requirement of the Education department – usually mentions the problems rather than detailing when school days ran smoothly! However, there were what read like endless hours and days of schooling lost for all manner of reasons.

Apart from the 'official' day off each year for the Sunday School outing to Weston-super-Mare – held in that era on a weekday - it was found impossible to compete with fairs and other events on Whiteshill Common or processions, led by bands, passing through the village. Typical of several entries in the log, one February, *'a wild beasts menagerie visited the neighbourhood and pitched their tents in the Common immediately opposite the school'*. The result was, *'a thin attendance in the pm'*.

The school had roughly the same holidays as we would recognise today, except for the summer holiday initially being called the Harvest holiday, reflecting the agricultural nature of the times. In the 1870s, the headmaster, Alfred Wallington, lamented the fact that half the children were still missing in September as they had to *'glean after the corn is housed'*.

Not long after, clearly exasperated, he further records that, *'Gleaning seems to be over and potato picking set in. It seems that there is hardly a clear month in the year when the children can attend with anything like regularity'*.

With roads almost non-existent, sometimes very wet weather made getting to school too difficult and there were a few occasions when the crowded school room became so hot in summer that the pupils were dismissed early. Until the Education Act of 1870, schooling was entirely optional, so some children were very irregular in their attendance, even if they came at all. This irregularity is witnessed by the 1869 Whiteshill school attendance record. The average number present was only 46 out of a school roll of 80 boys and girls.

From 1870 onwards, local school boards could make schooling compulsory for children aged between five and 13 but this did not become universal until ten years later. Despite being compulsory, some children were still kept away when their labourer fathers could not find work on the farms, leaving them with no money to pay the school fee of, by then, a penny or so a week per child.

Elementary schooling became free to every child in 1891 but non-attendance remained a problem regardless of the Attendance Officer chasing up, and in some cases issuing summonses on parents those children were habitually absent. The Whiteshill headmaster was known to sometimes send a pupil teacher to the houses of missing children to round them up.

Not doubting his concern for the absent children's education, he would also have been conscious of the fact that part of the school's Education department funding was based on the number of youngsters actually attending school each day – not the number of names on the school register.

It is no surprise that there were occasional cases of children being despatched to school by their parents but deciding to play truant. When found out, this was one of the few offences that merited use of the cane. The punishment meted out by Levi Luff in his time as headmaster was two strokes on each hand – at least in the case of boys; there seems to have been a reluctance to cane naughty girls, so they were usually kept in after school or deprived of the *'play hour'*.

Three boys who *'followed the hounds'* one day instead of attending school were spared the cane when Luff discovered that one of them had been given permission by his mother to skip school. Instead they were *'deprived of their recreation interval for a few days'*.

It was not unknown for a mother to ask, or indeed insist, that her child be caned by the headmaster! In one such incident Luff felt obliged to use the cane when a mother brought her daughter to him and reported the child's waywardness. Having applied the punishment, he had to intervene when the mother herself set about giving the girl a far more severe beating!

One of the other rare appearances of the cane was the result of stones being thrown by boys – and one hitting a teacher. Misdemeanours could lead to one stroke on each hand with a further stroke to the right hand if the miscreant had been untruthful about their offence. Generally, loss of play time or staying late after school was the standard punishment when needed – and in just a couple of cases over five decades, a persistently disruptive child was sent home and barred from the school.

Having been caught lighting fires on the Common opposite the school led to the culprits being verbally *'reproved'* and a boy lighting a fire in the cellar under the school appears to have been excused entirely - on the basis that he was only *'little'*!

So, corporal punishment was in no way the norm and a 'good talking to' with the possibility of their parents getting to hear of any misbehaviour was usually enough to deal with matters - not that keeping such a large number of children in order was the problem that we might today think it must have been. In later years being sent to stand on the 'penitence stool' (the one artefact that remains from the school) to bring an unruly pupil to their senses usually did the trick.

There were times when accidents disturbed school lessons - such as when, in 1899, a fire in the chapel heating *'apparatus'* meant quickly ripping out the schoolroom fireplace and pulling up the floorboards to prevent the blaze spreading. Or when sheets of glass fell out of a schoolroom skylight cutting one of the pupils, but fortunately not inflicting any serious injury.

The penitence stool - actually a chair with the back missing.

The worst accident happened directly outside the school in 1882 when pupil James Butler was crossing the road. Avoiding a carriage coming along the turnpike road he was hit and run over by the mail cart that came speeding through in the opposite direction. Two broken ribs and a pierced lung meant he was off school for a very long time – in fact it is unclear whether he was ever able to return to school.

By far the biggest 'stoppage' of schooling was caused by the prevalence of mumps, German measles, scarlatina [scarlet fever], chicken pox, whooping cough and diphtheria. In most years an outbreak of one or more of these nasty diseases among the pupils would lead to the school being shut for two or three weeks at a time on the instruction of Dr Crossman, the district medical officer of health and local GP who lived next to the church.

Sadly there were cases of pupils not surviving what were, in those days, deadly illnesses. This made parents wary about sending their children to school upon hearing the slightest whisper of a pupil being taken ill.

However, no school was immune from these epidemics so it did not affect the growth in pupil numbers at Whiteshill. In fact, one inspector put a less than usually good result of his visit down to the rapid intake of extra youngsters. Numbers rose to 100 by the end of the 1870s, carried on increasing over the next decade, and reaching an average attendance of 139.4 in 1891, the year in which school fees were done away with entirely.

Being an average attendance figure, this must have meant maybe 150 or more children often being squeezed into the two school rooms. When it was founded the school was registered with the British and Foreign School Society as able to accommodate up to 192 children while the government rules calling for only six square feet of space per pupil made it, in theory, plenty big enough for that number of pupils or even more!

Despite all that, in reality it was becoming apparent that by the standards of the end of the 19th Century, there was too little space for the number of pupils and the layout of the premises was getting outdated. School inspections began to flag up the need for more teaching staff – the school, as late as 1905 having only the headmaster, two certificated teachers, a pupil teacher and two 'paid monitresses'.

Maybe one sign of the premises becoming unsuitable for a school of this size was increasing mention of the *'unsatisfactory and insufficient offices'* - what today we call toilets. Unusual for a building with not even cesspit drainage until 1880 and no water supply until ten years after that, the toilets were inside the building – seemingly under the staircase to the upper school room. By the mid-1880s a few parents, fearful of *'insanitary conditions'* began moving their children to a different school.

To fix the problem as best they could, the church agreed to the school having a toilet put on the vestry side of the church for the boys. Over the next few years inspectors began to point out other shortcomings of the building, such as it having no playground and the skylights, the only windows and means of ventilation in the downstairs room, not being able to be opened when it was raining. The bad smell drifting through the building continued to be commented upon.

A visit in 1905 from Mr H W Household, Gloucestershire County Council Secretary for Education, (county councils now being responsible for local education[35]) marked the

---

[35] *The 1902 Education Act, introduced by the Conservative government, switched responsibility for education from local School Boards to Borough or County Councils with the cost of education being charged to ratepayers. Objections were numerous as the change took control away from local churches who had dominated the School Boards. On top of that, nonconformists were strongly opposed to paying (within their rates) to fund Church of England schools - which were by far the most numerous provider of elementary education. A nationwide civil disobedience campaign led to many thousands of ratepayers refusing to pay the education element of their rates demand. So great and long-lasting was the controversy, the 1902 Act is*

beginning of the end for the school. He was satisfied with the education being given, but again referred to the limitations of the building. His notebook recorded his opinion: *'Discipline in the school is very good and the attention is good. I questioned the top class in Arithmetic: I found rather unusual readiness and intelligence. The infants are being carefully pleasantly and intelligently taught'*.

But he felt obliged to note that the stairs down from the infants room *'are undeniably steep and awkward – two flights with a reverse turn'* and of the downstairs room, *'The ventilation on a wet day is probably very defective if all the lights have to be closed...and nothing can be done to the present school'*.

Within a few months, the county council Board of Education informed the school governors they were *'not prepared to extend their recognition of the premises'* beyond the end of February 1909. But as 1909 became all too close the council found themselves struggling to even secure a suitable site on which to build a replacement school.

A price could not be agreed for one local site and then the tenant of another potential piece of land, adjoining the nearby Star Inn, totally refused to have a school built on any part of the plot. Finally, in December 1908, a price of £265 was agreed for land on the opposite side of the Common from the church.

---

reckoned to have lost the Conservatives the General Election to the Liberals four years later. Rev George Jarvis, many years later the minister at Whiteshill but at that time a minister in Coleford, was one of a band of thirty who had belongings confiscated and sold in the town's market square by the County Council after refusing to pay the education element of their rates bill.

The Board of Education decided a temporary building should be put on the new plot straight away, to give time for plans to be drawn up for a permanent 200-pupil school. They were persuaded by their works sub-committee to abandon the idea of a temporary building but instead to extend the recognition of the church school, subject to erecting an emergency outside staircase from the upstairs schoolroom.

Where this staircase was situated and what it would achieve is difficult to think, however it was fitted just a

A group of pupils, photographed outside the chapel in the final year before moving across to the new council school. Headmaster Levi Luff is far right and far left is infants' teacher, Martha Pendock.

couple of days before the original deadline for closing the school.

It took almost two years to design, build and equip the new school. The Whiteshill day school finally closed on 22nd December 1910 for Christmas – and for ever! The managers provided a tea and entertainment for the pupils before they left and after Christmas the new council school opened with pupils transferring across to the new premises.

The day school mistresses and masters

Elizabeth Dennis is the earliest known mistress of Whiteshill day school and could have been in charge from the school first opening its doors to pupils in the early 1860s. She had been a pupil teacher from 1855 to 1860 at a school in her home town of Devonport.

Dennis had left the school by early 1870 to be replaced by Elizabeth Harwood who *'gave up charge of the school'* at the close of 1875 and was replaced by Alfred Wallington. He left in 1878 and married local girl Emma Pendock at Whiteshill chapel the following year, by which time he was a teacher in Lancashire. On a return visit in July 1880 the couple's first child, Ethel, was baptised at the chapel.

After the Easter of 1878 Harry Coward commenced as school master, at the same time as Emma's younger sister, Martha Pendock, took on the role of infants teacher, replacing Miss A Edwards who had held the position for a while. Coward had excelled during his two years at Borough Road College, where most British School masters trained, passing out with a First Class certificate.

He proved to be an outstanding teacher leading to him being poached from Whiteshill day school in November 1883, leaving at short notice to become head master of a Board school in Bristol. Coward transferred his church membership to Redland Park Congregational Church, near his new school.

He went on to head up Knowle School - at the time one of the largest in Bristol - for 20 years and was awarded an honorary degree from Bristol University for his work in the field of education and teacher training. He also became president of the National Union of Teachers.

After Coward left Whiteshill, George A Rice was brought in from Redcross Street British School in Bristol on an almost temporary basis, being replaced in September 1885 by 24 years old Levi Luff, the school's final and longest serving head.

Whiteshill school masters were active in the chapel as well as in the school with Luff being a prime example. Over his

Headmaster Levi Luff and wife Constance with the first staff of the new council school. Hilda Cleevely (far left) had attended the 'old' Whiteshill school from age three, as did most pupils. At 14 years old she became a paid monitress at the new school when it opened in 1911. (Hilda – married name Hibbard - attended the chapel throughout her life.)

years at Whiteshill he became Sunday School superintendent, a church deacon and church secretary. He transferred to the new Council school when it opened in January 1911, as did his wife Constance, by then a certificated assistant teacher.

Chapel reaches 50th anniversary

After two decades without a minister at Whiteshill, a new man was appointed - Rev Charles Knibbs - just in time for the chapel's 50th anniversary in the summer of 1866. A number of individuals had committed, between them, around £15 a quarter specifically towards a minister's salary. With the addition of a £2/10/0 quarterly contribution promised by the Congregational Union, the chapel was able to provide Knibbs with the reasonable, but not high salary of £25 a quarter.

Rev Charles Knibbs
Picture from Charles Lister Smith collection;
courtesy of Tom Round-Smith

Whiteshill would have been 27-year-old Knibbs' first pastorate after completing several years study at the newly established Bristol Theological Institute, a forerunner of the Congregationalists' Western College. Each of the ministers at Whiteshill over the next three-quarters of a century had trained for the ministry at one or other of these theological schools.

Not many weeks after his arrival the chapel's jubilee was celebrated with three meetings on Sunday 19th August 1866, followed by two more on the next day and finally a *'tea meeting'* on the Tuesday. The meetings must have been well supported if the amount given in the collections is anything to go by. The five offerings brought in a total of over £19 in addition to a profit of well over £8 from the tea, for which tickets were sold. In all, more than the minister's salary for three months!

Apparently, by this period the one remaining member of the chapel who had attended its opening was William Simmonds[36] [or Simmons], who was a deacon and treasurer in the early days and in 1856 had become a church trustee.

With a minister once again in place, the chapel's day school well established, and a thriving Sunday School, the church embarked on new activities as well as giving the building a major clean and re-paint, much of the cost being met by local gentleman (and for many years church treasurer) Jacob Dove.

Mothers' Meetings began as well as a Penny Reading club, both combining an element of *'mutual improvement'* (a popular concept for the working classes of the time) along with strong Christian teaching.

The mid-Victorian period saw the emergence of a wide variety of illustrated magazines. Penny Reading clubs read and discussed these as a means of broadening working class people's education, now that the ability to read was more common. It was usually the men who attended the Penny Reading sessions, but at Whiteshill we know, from surviving copies dated in the 1880s, such magazines, promoting Christianity and personal prudence, were also being read within the 80-strong Mothers' Meeting.

---

[36] *Simmonds was in the hat-making industry, an important source of employment locally, especially in Watleys End where in the 1840s it provided jobs for two-thirds of the men.*

The chapel was changing with the times in other ways as well. There was now a harmonium in the building so - assuming this was not used only by the Sunday School - singing 'a cappella' at services had given way to the use of musical accompaniment.

Weekly offerings and subscriptions were instituted - somehow in addition to the existing collections taken at morning and evening services once a month. It was not many years before most of the congregation had switched to weekly giving and the monthly collections were dispensed with in 1872. Weekly giving was by this time bringing in twice the amount coming from seat rents although the chapel still depended on various generous subscriptions, from a few better-off members and supporters, for nearly two-thirds of its income.

The brass candle holders were sold in 1866, the chapel's 50th year; lighting for the next half century being provided by oil lamps. The chapel began to make more use of its 'sexton', William Pritchard, to undertake various duties in and around the church, and in support of the minister. Reflecting this, his salary was doubled to £5 a year.

London-born Knibbs led the church for four years before accepting the call to a pastorate at Stonehouse in Gloucestershire.[37]

After Knibbs' departure from Whiteshill in the summer of 1870, Sunday services were conducted by Bristol Institute

---

[37] *In the first few months at Stonehouse Independent chapel Knibbs married his fiancée Alice Rushworth. Four years later they moved on to an Independent chapel in Torquay which had just been restored after a major fire. Knibbs died at the end of 1901 having been minister of the chapel for over 25 years and elected as President of the Devon Congregational Union.*

students for three months until 30-year-old Charles Eynon, another former Bristol Institute student, was called to become the chapel's next pastor.

Eynon, the eldest son of a brick-layer, was born and brought up just 60 miles away at Dymock in Gloucestershire. Prior to his time at Whiteshill he had spent a few years serving with the Bible Christian [38] ministry. He moved to Hambrook in the autumn of 1870, with his wife Lucy and their young baby daughter Flora - and Lucy only weeks away from giving birth to their second daughter, Annie.

Thus began a busy six years of ministry at the chapel, although Eynon was not formally ordained until 1873. Paid a little more than the previous minister, Eynon preferred not to accept the quarterly grant on offer from the Congregational Union.

Night school classes, public lectures and the formation of a Lodge of the grand-sounding Independent Order of Good Templars (IOGT) were added to the activities with which the church was already involved. The IOGT began in the

---

[38] *The Bible Christian Church, an off-shoot of the Wesleyan Methodist denomination, was formed in 1815 in North Cornwall. The church sent missionaries all over England and from the 1830s to many other countries. They made extensive use of female preachers but the most written-about Bible Christian preacher is probably Billy Bray, the unconventional Cornish preacher whose sermons were often enlivened by spontaneous outbursts of singing and dancing.*

United States in 1851 aimed at *'enlightening people around the world on a lifestyle free from alcohol and other drugs'.*[39]

The first of many English lodges was founded in 1868 and the Whiteshill church lodge was up and running by 1873 reflecting Lucy and Charles Eynon's staunch advocacy of temperance and total abstinence.

The church day school, for which, as minister, Eynon was secretary of the managers, would have been another interest shared with his wife, Lucy having been a pupil teacher in her home town of Crediton during her teenage years[40]. Lucy sometimes joined her husband when he paid his regular visits to check on the running of the school and confirm the attendance register had been correctly marked.

1872 marked the first year on record that the chapel had a Christmas tree. It was laden with gifts supplied and then bought by members of the congregation. (Christmas trees had become popular in England after Prince Albert, Queen Victoria's husband, set one up in Windsor Castle in 1841.) Carol singing in the area was introduced a couple of Decembers later.

---

[39] *The IOGT had spread worldwide by the end of the 19th Century and still exists today, with its headquarters in Stockholm, Sweden. In the 1970s, in an attempt to modernise its image IOGT changed some of its titles and ritualistic features that had originally been modelled on those of the Freemasons, although admitting both men and women of all races from its earliest days.*

[40] *Three of Lucy's children became teachers; Flora, Rosa who ran her own kindergarten and Kate who was a teacher in South Africa.*

The pulpit - lower than when originally installed.

In a leaflet written for the chapel's 100th anniversary in 1916, it is said that during Eynon's ministry the first pipe organ was installed, the church *'re-seated'* and the pulpit, which was much higher up when installed in 1816, lowered to the height at which it stands today. It was mounted onto a *'rostrum'* which can clearly be seen to be of a different wood from the pulpit itself.

Part or all of the changes must have been undertaken in the summer of 1872 as *'alterations being made in chapel'* necessitated

Today's pews might well be the ones installed in the 1870s but they have certainly been repositioned more than once in later years.

closing the adjoining day school for several days, according to the school log.

The Western Daily Press reported in early 1875 that, *'Rev C Eynon has intimated his intention of resigning the pastorate of Whiteshill Congregational Church'*, but whether or not this report was correct, Eynon continued as minister for another 18 months.

While at Whiteshill the Eynon's family grew apace – with the birth of three more daughters, then two sons – all within the course of less than six years. Sadly, with their second son, Sidney, only a few months old, Charles Eynon died on 16th September 1876, at only 36 years of age. An obituary in one of the Bristol papers spoke of him *'having been ill for about three weeks, but it was hoped that he was recovering, and his death at last was sudden.'*

We do know that visiting speakers were brought in each Sunday, from some months before his death and his last, previously frequent visit to the church school was in mid-June 1876, so his period of illness could have been longer than reported.

Left a widow in her early thirties and with six children to raise - ranging in age from a few months to six years old - Lucy was paid the salary due to her husband to the date of his death and in the November was presented with the sum of £21 collected by *'the Church, Congregation & Sunday School'*.

Obviously a women of some resolve, she moved to Westbury-on-Trym and before long was employed as a *'mission visitor'* for a local church and tended to her children with the help of a live-in governess. Lucy Eynon was living in South London by the start of the 20th Century working as the paid organiser of the Women's Total Abstinence Society and she journeyed back to the chapel at Whiteshill now and again, to speak on the subject.

More people than seats!

In the months following the untimely death of Whiteshill minister Charles Eynon in 1876, senior deacon Thomas Edwards turned to the Wesleyan Methodists to *'supply the pulpits at 2/- each Sunday from Bristol and back'*. But this was only a 'stop-gap' while he visited wealthy local Congregationalists to seek promises of funding towards the salary of a new pastor.

Subscriptions pledged for at least two years, were enough

Rev William Porter

for the church to feel able to invite William John Porter to become the next Whiteshill minister. Not quite 23 years old, Porter, the youngest pastor the church has ever had, was selected from a number of candidates sent to preach by the Bristol Theological Institute.

His ministry began in mid-1877 and after a satisfactory probationary year the Institute sanctioned his ordination the following Autumn. During his time at Whiteshill the church became full to overflowing, with a waiting list of those who wanted to reserve their place at services by paying a half-yearly seat rent!

The number listed as church members climbed steadily from just under 50 to nearly 120 during his nine years as pastor. The Sunday congregation, particularly in the evening service, must have been twice that number and 75 regularly attended the Thursday evening *'Pastor's Bible Class'*. Each year there was a steady flow of new converts - *'those who have come to Christ'* - plus transfers from other churches of new people moving into the locality; more than offsetting the loss of those who had been *'taken to the Church of the First-born'*, as the pastor phrased their passing.

Members were active in distributing tracts around the district, led by Whiteshill day school master and church member Harry Coward for several years. Inside the church there were mutual improvement classes, singing classes (also run by Coward) and a Coal & Light Club – maybe some sort of meeting to encourage Christian thriftiness and the saving of money for household expenses, such as the winter coal.

Thomas Moreman, a well-known blind evangelist from Kingswood, Bristol, was asked to come and conduct a week of special meetings, preceded by three evenings of prayer. It resulted in conversions, with the pastor urging upon the church, *'the necessity of earnest prayer on behalf of those who had recently given their hearts to Christ'*. At nearly every monthly members' business meeting, names were mentioned of those who were to be interviewed for membership of the church.

These years of strong church growth made fitting everyone in for services a continual issue. Several ideas were proposed for squeezing in extra seats to accommodate the large number of people attending Sunday services – and in particular those who wanted to pay to rent a seat! It was even suggested that the organ be moved up into the gallery [balcony] to make space for 17 extra seats that could be 'rented out.'

A more feasible solution was adopted; part of the gallery was equipped with better seats, suitable for renting, as until then, it seems the gallery had only benches with no backs. Room was found for some seats behind the choir and choir members were asked to give up the rented seats many of them held in the main body of the church in favour of reserved seats in the choir stalls.

It was decided in 1879 to make major changes to the seating arrangements although the economic difficulties being encountered across the country, in part due to several years of bad weather, made paying for the changes a real concern. *'Altering the seats in the chapel'* was postponed *'for a few months, as probably the depression in trade will not be as great and the prospect of being able to meet the expenses incurred will be better'.* It was agreed to sell tickets for two or three concerts and a winter lecture or two to cover the cost.

The Sunday School remained strong and in addition a 'Band of Hope'[41] grew to attract 150 under 16 year-olds. Part of a national organisation, its objective was to teach children the importance and principles of alcoholic abstinence from a Christian perspective. The Total Abstinence movement had started nearly half a century

---

[41] *The Band of Hope was founded by a Baptist minister in 1847. It advocated and taught sobriety and teetotalism. In 1855, a national organisation was formed and meetings were held in churches throughout the UK providing activities for children that encouraged them to avoid alcohol problems. 'Signing the pledge' - a promise not to drink alcohol - was one of the innovative features and millions of people signed up. The movement steadily grew to nearly three million members by 1935. By the early 1950s, however, the temperance movement had all but succumbed to a changing society and cultural habits.*

earlier in disgust at the 1832 'Beer Act' which led to thousands of beer-houses springing up almost overnight.

The Church of England and the Quakers were early supporters of the movement. Independent or Congregational churches, like Whiteshill, were generally apathetic, many concurring with the view that, *'We are not prepared to submit to censure for the temperate use of that which we regard to be one of the choice blessings of a beneficent Creator'*.

Decanters of wine continued to be on the platform of their public religious meetings and there was a universal custom of offering wine to the preacher on his descent from the pulpit after Sunday services – as happened at Whiteshill chapel until at least the mid-1840s and maybe much later.

However, growing support for the temperance movement in individual congregations over the years finally saw the Congregational Union swing into full-hearted support by 1860.

The question of using alcoholic wine for Communion troubled many but the issue did not come to a head at Whiteshill for another 30 years, when, after discussion, a church meeting voted in favour of continuing with the use of *'slightly intoxicating wine'* – only to change its mind the next month, by accepting the offer of several members to supply their homemade non-intoxicating wine for communion.

During Porter's time at Whiteshill as well as alterations to the inside of the building he introduced changes in the worship services. US soloist and composer Ira Sankey was making a new style of gospel song extremely popular through singing to huge audiences at revival meetings in Britain with evangelist Dwight L Moody.

This led Porter to obtain one of Sankey's earliest song books for use at Whiteshill. Later Porter also started to use hymns from the recently published, *'Supplement to the Congregational Hymn Book'*. Members were expected to buy their own copy, although it was agreed that *'poor members of the Congregation be supplied from the incidental fund'*.

It was decided that anyone applying for membership should be interviewed by the pastor at his home – not by two church members as had previously happened. And new members would be received into membership at *'sacramental'* services, no longer at church members' business meetings.

The earliest surviving written record of church members, baptisms, marriages and minutes of business meetings - in a specially produced book bought from the Congregational Union – dates from the time of Porter's ministry[42].

Many of the changes and improvements to the church building in the 1880s were thanks to the generosity of Henry Derham - one of the local Congregationalists whose earlier offers of funding had given the church the confidence to invite Porter to become pastor. Derham was a partner in his family's Bristol-based wholesale shoe and boot manufacturing business employing 2,000 people.

---

[42] *In the chapel's first couple of decades very important matters were simply written up on spare pages in the church financial accounts book. Then a 'church book' was purchased in 1833 – maybe significantly, the very same year as the chapel, for some unknown reason, re-registered its existence. The church book might have been to record membership, baptisms and member's meeting minutes over the next few decades but as it is not amongst the church records that exist today this can be no more than supposition.*

He had recently moved into the Manor House in Frenchay with his wife, four or more children and six servants (parlour maid, housemaid, under-housemaid, nurse maid, cook and kitchen maid) – plus husband & wife coachman & dressmaker and a gardener's family, in lodges in the estate grounds.

The Manor House Frenchay - during the Derham's occupancy it would have been a horse-drawn carriage outside, not a car!

Derham and his wife Emma decided to transfer from Arley Chapel in Bristol, becoming members at Whiteshill in 1879 and just under a year later, Thomas Edwards stood down as senior deacon (sometimes called church secretary) in favour of Henry Derham. Sadly, Emma Derham died under 18 months later at only 40 years-of-age. In May 1883 Henry Derham remarried, his new wife, aged 19 years old, becoming a church member later the same year and immediately being expected to take prime position on the ladies committee that organised various church events.

Also in 1883 Derham offered to pay for new oil lamps throughout the church building, superseding the older type which were frequently needing to have their glass replaced. At the same time the interior of the chapel was refurbished. (There was another renovation six years later including re-securing the cornice around the edge of the ceiling, it having been '*in a dangerous state*' for some time.)

New '*hot air apparatus*' was installed at a cost of £40 in 1884, not that everyone was convinced it generated the warmth the old stove had provided. The stove was offered to the day school for the school room and two more seats were fitted in where it had stood in the church. Almost all the cost of the refurbishment and of the new heating system was contributed by Derham's firm or by Derham personally.

Henry Freeman, one of the four deacons of the period, had been church organist for some years. He moved away from the district in May 1884 so Derham's 19-years-old daughter Beatrice took over – and also formed and conducted a church choir which had obviously not continued from its earlier days. The organ was badly in need of repair and three options were considered: repairing the organ at a cost of £5, having an entirely new organ made at a cost of £180, or the building of a new organ but using a few parts from the old one.

The current pipe organ was largely funded by church secretary Henry Derham and his family in the 1880s.

The estimate of £140 for the latter option was readily accepted when the Derham family offered to cover most of the cost. (A thorough overhaul of the organ in 2008 brought to light evidence that some of the pipes might have been the items re-used from the previous instrument.) Henry Derham gave £50, his young sons £50, his daughters £20 and 11 other members, one of them the pastor, between them pledged the final £20. The organ, built by eminent Bristol organ builders W G Vowles, was in use the following year - as it has been ever since.

By the time the new organ was installed Beatrice had resigned as organist, possibly looking ahead to her marriage (at Whiteshill) in the summer of 1886. However, according to the records another Miss Derham took over. This would have been Beatrice's younger sister Blanche, who had been accepted into membership of the church in mid-1884.

Henry Derham led a busy life - active in the church, in his family business, in politics and in civic life. By 1884 he was not a well man and the following October, 'suffering from severe illness, under orders from advisers', he sailed off on a P&O steamer bound for India, Australia and New Zealand. The many-months-long rest cure appears to have restored him to good health, although whether he made it as restful as his doctors prescribed is open to question, looking at the reports he filed to the Bristol newspapers from ports in Colombo, India, Hong Kong, Canton and Japan!

Edwards had readily stood down from his long-time role of church secretary back in 1880 when Derham came on the scene as he felt he was filling too many 'offices' in the church, among other things being superintendent of the very large Sunday School. He continued to serve as one of four church deacons but the year was not out before he had accepted yet another role; that of church treasurer, a post being relinquished by William Simmonds 'who had long and successfully filled the office'.

By 1885 Edwards considered it was time to relinquish both the position of treasurer and of deacon, thus bringing onto prominence another local family; the Doves. A successful leather merchant and local gentleman of considerable standing, Jacob Dove was already a strong supporter of both the church and its day school, and lived just down the road from the chapel, in Hambrook House.

Jacob Dove served as treasurer and deacon for the next 18 years. (He was followed by his son Frederick Dove for 38 years, and after him by his grandson Philip Dove who oversaw the finances until 1973; totalling not far off 90 years 'looking after the books' across the three generations.)

Jacob Dove's wife, Mary and the minister's wife, Lydia Porter, some 15 years younger, were born in the same area of Norfolk and they shared the unusual maiden name – Weasenham. Although there was, and is, a small parish of Weasenham All Saints in Norfolk, few Victorian census records show it as a surname. Could it be that the two wives were related? Whether or not the case, there was definitely a family connection many years later, when one of Jacob Dove's sons, Frank, married the Porter's daughter, Grace[43].

Grace was the Porters' eldest child, born in 1880. Next came a son, Gerald, in 1882 and another daughter, Beatrice about a year later. No doubt Elizabeth, their 14 years old live-in domestic servant - a feature of home life for ministers of the period - was kept busy helping with the young family. Lydia was expecting a fourth child, John, as the family

---

[43] *Grace and Frank would have known each other from chapel but certainly <u>not</u> through attending the Whiteshill day school! Both sets of parents were strong supporters of the school but prevailing class distinctions meant there would have been no question of either of them sending their own children there. Grace was sent to Milton Mount College from when she was 10 or 11 years-of-age. This sizable boarding school outside Gravesend in Kent catered exclusively for daughters of Congregational ministers. At the same time as Grace began her years as one of the school's 140 pupils, 17 years old Kate Eynon, daughter of Whiteshill's previous minister, was one of its three student teachers, most likely continuing on from having been a pupil at the school.*

moved on from Whiteshill, William Porter having accepted the call to the pastorate of France Chapel in Chalford Hill, near Stroud in Gloucestershire[44].

In a glowing address given at his valedictory service on the last day of March 1886, it was said of Porter he had, *'preached the Gospel, quickened the careless, sustaining and strengthening God's own people'.* The family was presented with *'a handsome and costly Dining Table from the Church & Congregation, three volumes of Shakespeare and a beautiful edition of Tennyson, with photographs, by the Sunday School and Bible Class, a handsome table from the Mothers' Meeting and a massive inkstand, letter scales and blotter by the Band of Hope'.*

---

[44] *Porter's wife Lydia died in 1896 aged only 40. In the same year William Porter moved on to pastor Tyndale Congregational church in Gloucester where he led a flourishing church that opened mission halls in other parts of the city and in his time the church was reckoned to run the largest Sunday School in Gloucester. He stayed for 20 years before retiring from the ministry. A couple of years into this pastorate Porter married again, to Gratianna Dixon, who had moved back from the Home Counties having herself been left widowed with several children at a relatively young age.*

Unrest in the gallery, changes at the organ

The problem of squeezing all those into the chapel who wanted to attend Sunday evening services continued under the next minister, Rev Thomas Owen Prosser, who arrived eight months after his predecessor, Porter, left in the Spring of 1886. Numbers dropped off a little in the period the chapel was without a minister but by the end of Prosser's three years at Whiteshill a steady flow of new people, some as the result of another series of special meetings conducted by evangelist Thomas Moreman, brought the congregation close to the numbers seen in the previous years.

Prosser came to Whiteshill as a result of the church asking the Bristol Theological Institute to send four of its *'oldest and best'* students, each to conduct services for a Sunday morning and evening. In fact, from these visits the church initially invited to the pastorate a man about to finish his training – George Jarvis. He declined the offer, deciding instead to accept a call from a church in Stonehouse, Gloucestershire, but returned a quarter of a century later to serve for nearly 20 years as Whiteshill's pastor.

The congregation looked to another of the students sent to preach – Thomas Prosser, a 26 year-old Welshman from the Brecons, but he hesitated, being still many months short of completing his training at the Institute.

Letters went to and fro until satisfactory arrangements were agreed for him to be provided by the church with horse or carriage transport to Bristol to attend lectures while starting to undertake duties at Whiteshill on a probationary basis. This being settled, Prosser's ministry at the chapel commenced that December but he was not ordained until over 12 months later, having completed his studies.

In this era, the well-attended Sunday services were not necessarily without their challenges for the pastor and his sexton, John Player, as they dealt with *'the [bad] conduct of the young men in the gallery'*. The *'ringleaders'* had to be given a good talking to by the sexton. At other times Prosser had to bring up the subject of children's behaviour. He *'thought something more should be done in order that stillness may be secured on the gallery'* so a few members, rather reluctantly agreed to sit with the children in the gallery.

Then there were members of the congregation who, having paid to rent a specific seat, thought nothing of arriving well after the start of services – thereby leaving seats unoccupied, to the irritation of those the sexton was having to make stand at the back of the chapel, in the absence of any vacant 'free' seats.

It was decided that rented seats would only be reserved until 6pm, the start time of the evening service, but this did not go down well with some of those who rented seats and in the end was not carried out except where individual seat holders agreed. On more than one occasion Prosser was driven to make *'a few remarks respecting the individual duties of members as to punctuality'*.

For a time, the sexton was given the assistance of two more members to help seat people for the evening service. To ease the situation further two other members were stationed outside the doors of the church to welcome *'strangers'*. Around the same period, for reasons that are not stated in the records, the morning service was changed from 10.30 to 10.45 am.

Church finances were generally satisfactory, in no small part due to the generosity of church secretary Henry Derham and Jacob Dove, the treasurer, but the pair did expect others to make a contribution, within their means, to the expenses of the church. The minimum charge for renting a seat was increased to 1/6d a quarter and as Dove pointed out at a church members' meeting, a good number of the congregation could be expected to afford this, it equating to only one-and-a-half pennies a week.

The congregation was encouraged to consider using the weekly offering envelopes which had first been introduced in the early 1880s (and continued for the next seven decades) as an alternative to the weekly collection taken up at services.

Both forms of weekly giving plus special offerings taken up from time-to-time were raising an increasing amount but still much less than subscriptions - from a very small number of the congregation - plus seat rents, which were gradually dying out. It was not to be until the mid-1890s that freewill offerings became greater than income from individual subscriptions and by a decade beyond that, offerings constituted two-thirds of church income.

Now and again collections were taken at the door after Sunday services, but only for special purposes such as in support of the Congregational Union Church Aid Fund or once a year for the day school. Having a collection at the monthly 'sacramental service' [Communion] was still the practice of the church, but as had always been the case, this money was used by the pastor for relief of the poor in the district.

'Public Teas' provided one of the chapel's important means of income. These had long been held on the Monday after Harvest Thanksgiving and the Monday after the Church

Anniversary services. They would be followed by a *'Public Service'* – a visiting speaker giving what was called a *'lecture'* – a sermon by any other name. Sometimes, on a Whitsun Monday, a tea would be followed by *'entertainment'* but not as we might understand that term today. Tickets to a tea would cost 6d or maybe 9d with catering arranged for 100 or 120 people.

The late 1880s saw the start of additional teas, one each quarter, at the suggestion of a newly formed finance committee. Around the same time, maybe at the instigation of the same people, special Sunday collections, presumably a retiring offering in addition to the normal weekly collection, were taken up once a quarter for chapel funds. Some of the congregation also gave a regular sum towards funding missionary work, these subscriptions totalling well over £20 a year.

'Xmas Bazaars', a lucrative feature of church life for many years, were held a day or two after Boxing Day. Derham, the church secretary, objected to them on principle, maintaining they led to *'disorderly conduct'*. Despite his strong influence over everything that happened at the chapel, members were not prepared to forgo the bazaar, especially as it made a profit of over £15 for chapel funds, but its name was tactfully changed to *'A Xmas Tree and Sale of Work'* for a year or two.

Needless to say, although Mrs Derham led the ladies committee who organised teas and other such events she kept well away from organising bazaars!

Over the course of three or four years there were several changes of chapel organist, some recruited - for the first time - from outside the church and paid for playing at Sunday services. Blanche Derham had proved a capable and keen church organist but was often away from the district, maybe with her father Henry Derham, who was by now travelling far and wide in connection with his international footwear business.

Not long before Prosser arrived, there had been a collection at one Sunday's services to fund Elton Thatcher, an accomplished local organist, to fill in during Blanche's absences and another musician was asked to preside at the organ, for 5/- a day, when neither was available. Hoping for a more settled arrangement, the next year a Mr Drew of Frampton became the 'full time' organist with a stipend of £15 a year towards which Dove and Derham promised £8, the remaining £7 coming from a collection.

Drew did not stay many months so the post had to be advertised and in came another paid organist, Mr Woodcock - who lasted little longer than his predecessor before asking to be released. This time the church looked within its own number for a replacement and asked a Miss Hill, one of a family who were church members, to play at services for three months, at the end of which she was persuaded to continue, as she did, very satisfactorily, for several years.

A link with the history of the chapel that went back to its very formation was broken in 1888 when one of the church trustees, Joseph Foster died. His father John Foster had been one of the chapel's founding trustees and his father-in-law had been John Godwin, another of the original trustees, who had written off the chapel's building debt back in 1821. A *black mourning cloth* was placed on the pulpit to testify to *the respect and esteem* in which Joseph Foster, who had been a good friend to the chapel, was held.

Prosser served ably as Whiteshill pastor for three years – almost to the day – leaving to pastor a Congregational church in Halstead, Essex at the end of November 1889[45]. He is recorded as having discharged his duties in an '*able, loving and elegant manner*' and judging by his farewell gifts after a relatively short ministry his talents must have been thoroughly appreciated.

He was presented with a '*beautiful and costly writing desk mounted with an engraved silver plate, a handsome and expensive study chair accompanied by a beautiful cushion*' and from the Mothers Meeting a '*large and elegant duplex lamp for study with two vases to match*'.

---

[45] *Prosser later held pastorates in Devizes in Wiltshire, Deal in Kent and Fulwood in Yorkshire. He died in 1932 and is buried in Downend Cemetery, Bristol, along with his wife who came from the city.*

Change and tragedy

The early months of 1890 were a time of change for Whiteshill; a new minister, departure of a much respected church secretary and ... running water piped in to a tap in the chapel yard - the cost of the latter shared with the day school. The church had only been a couple of months without a pastor before, fresh out of Bristol Theological Institute, Henry Alban Brown, a 27-year-old Welshman from Haverfordwest in Pembrokeshire, arrived on the scene.

Rev Henry Alban Brown

Being single, who better to board with than Levi and Constance Luff? Levi was headmaster of Whiteshill day school for which, as pastor, Brown would be taking management responsibility as chairman of the school committee. What neither could have known at the time was that Luff would soon be asked to take over as church secretary.

In April 1890, a couple of weeks before the *'Public Recognition Tea and Service'* to mark the start of Brown's ministry, the congregation learnt that Henry Derham, who was such a driving force in the life of the church, as well as its major benefactor, would be stepping down from his roles as church secretary and deacon.

Derham's father, James, the last of the two founding brothers of wholesale shoe and boot makers' Derham Bros., had died a few weeks earlier. Henry Derham inherited the family estate in Bristol's Sneyd Park so would be moving from Frenchay[46]. After Derham's departure, the church begged his services for several years to chair chapel meetings where notable speakers had been invited to preach.

He continued, for a while at least, to preside over monthly meetings of the Liberal Association in the schoolroom.[47] For the children of the church his move to Bristol deprived them of the pleasure of picnics in the extensive grounds – 110 acres - of his home, Frenchay Manor, that, for several years, had followed on from the annual Sunday School outing to Weston-super-Mare.

One thing that did not change with the arrival of the new minister was *the behaviour of the children in the gallery'* during services! Brown went further than previous ministers by suggesting the youngsters should be allowed to leave before the sermon for a short service of their own in the schoolroom. The members were not ready for what

---

[46] *Henry Derham became Managing Director of Derham Bros, one of the largest companies in the City of Bristol. He and his family transferred their membership to the Congregational church in Sneyd Park. He continued as a Justice of the Peace but, with increased business commitments, stood down from being a Gloucestershire County Council Alderman in 1892.*

[47] *Henry Derham was always active in local politics. During his time at Whiteshill he had borrowed the school rooms for special Liberal Party meetings – sometimes the pupils being sent home early so the room could be readied for the evening's event. The formation of the Hambrook and District Liberal Association, of which Derham was the chairman, was one such occasion as was an address in 1890 by Member of Parliament (and Whiteshill chapel trustee) Handel Cossham on an issue of the day.*

they saw as a radical proposal so, as on previous occasions, opted for asking *'teachers and friends'* to sit in the gallery with the children.

When that did not cure the problem it was decided the children should be moved downstairs from the balcony to the side of the chapel nearest the vestry *'and that any Seat-holders who might thus be inconvenienced be seen and asked to kindly acquiesce in the arrangement'*.

Despite Brown's proposal for a separate children's service not finding favour, he proved to be an extremely enthusiastic, capable and well-respected pastor, alongside playing an active role in the community as a member, and then chairman, of the parish council. Over and above the well-attended Sunday services, there was hardly an evening of the week when church members were *'not engaged in some good work.'*

He set about reviving the Band of Hope for the youngsters, which had fallen away over the previous few years while the adults were encouraged to be fully committed and involved in the temperance movement, attending local rallies or marches and sending delegates to mass public meetings in the Colston Hall.

The beginning-of-year *'social meetings'* of this era – comprising reports on church activity mixed with solos, recitations and sacred music recitals (and later, for the first time, free refreshments!) – heard of a Sunday School bulging at the seams, and extra week-night activities. These were a Young People's Christian Band [not the musical type!], a Watchers' Band (the prayer Union of the London Missionary Society), IBRA meetings (International Bible Reading Association) and involvement in the local Free Church Girl's Guild.

All this was over and above week-night worship and prayer services plus activities that continued from earlier times, such as the Mutual Improvement meetings; now occasionally including the novelty of lectures accompanied by projected *'limelight views'*[48] - not that the Sunday School missed out on this new technology either. In December 1892 the church approved *'a Lantern Exhibition of a Religious and instructive nature to be given to the children and their friends'*, but not on a Sunday!

No wonder church business meetings had to be squeezed in after one or another of the week-night meetings finished, and, maybe surprisingly in light of the respect with which the Sabbath was treated, sometimes church business was discussed after the sacramental service on a Sunday evening.

Services and other activities continued to be well supported during this period, notwithstanding numbers being affected in the mid-1890s through some families moving away from the district and quite a number of older members dying.

One notable death at the close of 1897 was of Thomas Edwards [49] who had retired as Sunday School

---

[48] *Picture slides projected by a 'magic lantern' using an oxyhydrogen flame directed at a cylinder of quicklime to produce an intense illumination – in the days before electric light.*

[49] *Thomas Edwards, like his father James, had trained and worked as a cordwainer (shoemaker) but by the 1870s was running a grocery store and drapers on the main road – the turnpike road – in Hambrook. He also later went into market gardening with his youngest son, Albert – doubtless selling the produce through his shop. Thomas and his wife Ann had always lived in the locality but after Thomas died Ann moved to Yorkshire to live with daughter Amelia and her husband.*

superintendent several years earlier after a connection with the children's work that went back 44 years. He had been a church trustee since 1856, senior deacon in the 1870s and for several years chapel treasurer. His role of Sunday School superintendent was taken over by Levi Luff – on top of him being church secretary, a deacon and headmaster of the day school.

New people joined the church in small numbers each year, generally transferring from other churches. The exception was 1901 when conversions resulting from special evangelistic services led to the names of 14 candidates for membership being brought before just one of the year's church meetings.

The annual round of *'public teas'* to raise funds, followed by *'public lectures'* continued to be used to deal with the financial deficits that were encountered each year, especially now that Derham's generosity was no longer available to the chapel and even more so after the death in 1902 of the other prime chapel benefactor, Jacob Dove.

The chapel's tight financial position did not quench the congregation's commendable desire to contribute to good causes such as the up-grading of Dr Crossman's Hambrook village cottage hospital – of which Brown was on the steering committee; the Bristol Royal Infirmary and the London Missionary Society to name but three of many beneficiaries of special Sunday collections.

One-off donations and funds generated from staging well-attended organ concerts of sacred music and *'social entertainment'* evenings helped provide the means to keep the building in reasonable shape – including the interior walls being cleaned and repainted in their traditional green colour and a new chimney being built to try to improve the heating system.

The Christmas bazaar still served to wipe out any annual overspend at most year ends, although they were not to everyone's liking; some members pledging subscriptions only on condition that no bazaar would be held.

Brown instituted a large committee of men and women to run most church affairs and appears to have reduced the frequency and subject matter of member's meetings. Much of the deacons' previous role in decision-making passed to this committee, probably with Brown personally managing issues bearing on the spiritual life of the church

The church started sending delegates fairly regularly to meetings of the Bristol, Gloucester and Hereford District Association of the Congregational Union. In 1892 the district association annual meetings were held at Whiteshill and in October 1903 the Autumnal meeting took place at the chapel.

In 1892 two ladies, Maria Elliott and her sister Mary, 13 years her senior, were received into membership at Whiteshill. Qualified teachers, they had previously run a small boarding school for girls in Bristol but now lived in Hambrook.

The sisters threw themselves wholeheartedly into the work of the church running various evening activities, entertaining local children in their home for Bible study, serving on the 'tea' committee and in the case of Mary joining the management committee of the Whiteshill day school. Maria was nominated as the chapel representative, along with the pastor, on the Bristol Missionary Society committee.

Maria being 16 years older than Brown did not stop a strong affection growing between the two, leading to their marriage being celebrated at the chapel in July 1894. The ceremony was conducted by Alban Brown's brother John, a Congregational minister across in Penarth, South Wales. Married life suited the couple but in the final couple of years of his 16 year ministry, Brown suffered from bouts of ill-health and in particular a difficulty in concentrating.

In April 1904 Brown felt he had *'to ask the Church to allow him a few Sundays of freedom from pulpit work'* part of which to be considered his normal one month's annual holiday. In the event, visiting speakers had to be arranged for the whole of the rest of the year. Brown was a keen and able organist and although not feeling able to lead or preach at services he was happy and willing to play, with Elton Thatcher being employed to assist. After a while Thatcher resigned, finding that sharing organ-playing with Brown in services was not a workable arrangement.

Effectively left without a pastor for over two years the church officers were reluctant to seek a replacement, praying that Brown's health would improve so he could pick up the role again. By 1906, rather than any improvement, Brown's condition had deteriorated. His strange and distracted behaviour was being noticed and commented on by the congregation and other local people alike.

Obviously, Maria was deeply concerned about her husband's increasing depression and hoped that getting away to take in the sea-air might restore his health as it had in the past. This was not to be and finally, in the most tragic moment in the history of the church, on 30th July 1906 while at their home, Brown, normally a gentle man, murdered his wife, her sister Mary who lived with them and then committed suicide. The shock to congregation and community can be imagined. People came from surrounding villages just to stand outside the house where the multiple tragedy had occurred.

Writing in the church record book a year later and clearly still affected by the horrific events in a family to which he and his wife had been particularly close, church secretary Levi Luff apologised for not having kept the minute book up-to-date since the events of July 1906.

He wrote of the pastor's years of bad health and lamented the fact that Brown had ended his life *'in a manner from which we all shrink to recall'* but nevertheless wished to place on record *'the Christlike character & spirit in which his whole life had been lived & which makes the sad end one of the great mysteries, the solution of which we must await in the great Beyond'*.

Into the 20th Century

It is no surprise that the church endured difficult times in the aftermath of the drama of July 1906. It was fully accepted that Brown had acted completely out of character as a result of a longstanding medical problem but nevertheless, the tragedy had its effect on numbers attending the church. Income from offerings and seat rents dipped somewhat, not starting to pick up again until after the First World War.

Stunned by the terrible events, the church sought advice from the Congregational Union and the Principal of Western College before cautiously starting the hunt for a new pastor. Previous ministers Prosser and Porter suggested several names but each one looked at was either not in a position to take up the vacancy or not considered suitable by the membership. Church secretary Luff was kept busy booking visiting speakers to fill the pulpit on Sundays for the next year and a half.

The large business committee set up by Brown was replaced with six elected deacons. Leaning strongly on the Congregational Union at this time, the church took to paying a subscription annually to the district and the national Union. From 1907 until the First World War both annual subscriptions were made and after that only the one to the district Union.[50]

---

[50] *Congregational churches were encouraged to pay 10/6d a year to the district association and 10/- a year to the national Union, however being a denomination of independent churches these subscriptions were not obligatory and, like Whiteshill to this point, many chose not to contribute.*

Indicating the great respect in which many in the church still held their previous minister, members called for a lasting memorial to Alban Brown. Suggestions of a wall plaque or upgrading of the organ, which he had loved to play, were trumped by the imaginative idea of church deacon Thomas Bridgeman Pendock to have built, in Brown's memory, a manse for future pastors. Moreover he offered to donate a plot of land on which it could be built.

With plans drawn up by June 1909 came the realisation the £250 that had been raised was only half of what was needed! Not to be put off, Pendock offered to sell Holmelea, a property he owned in Hambrook *'for the moderate sum of £330'* of which he would give back £50 in lieu of the site he had originally offered. Then things moved very fast – as an immediate purchase was going to save £1/10/0 in stamp fees.

The financial shortfall of £30 was borrowed until that amount could be raised, allowing the purchase to be completed in a matter of weeks. Renamed 'The Memorial

A sketch of the memorial manse made soon after it was purchased in 1909.

Manse'[51] , the cottage provided a home for successive Whiteshill ministers until a replacement manse was built nearby 40 years later.

A year after Alban Brown's death his brother, Rev John Brown, suggested a friend of his, Rev George Henry Lea, as a potential pastor for Whiteshill. Still moving cautiously, the deacons visited the Chief Constable of Bristol who had been a deacon at Lodge Street Chapel when Lea had been a member there, to *'hear his testimony'* before recommending Lea to the membership.

The church voted in favour of calling Lea but had to accept the new minister could not fill the vacant post until the beginning of 1908 due to his existing commitment overseas.

In contrast to most previous Whiteshill pastors who were young men fresh from theological training, the new pastor was in his fifties having served with the London Missionary Society in Tanganyika and in Jamaica over a span of some 14 years. In addition he had experience of leading churches in England. He was originally from Leeds but his wife, Emily, was born in Bristol. On Rev John Brown's advice, Lea came initially for one year, on a salary of £100, but in the event stayed for nearer four.

For reasons not spelt out in the church meeting minutes two of the six deacons resigned as deacons midway through Lea's time as pastor, not that it stopped the members asking Lea to stay on at the close of his 12 months contract and again when he proposed leaving in April 1910 - after which he remained a further year.

-----

[51] *Holmelea, situated between the church and the ring road, on the right by Simmonds Yard, now goes under the name, 'The Old Manse'.*

Volunteers had been found to fill the posts and lead the activities for which Maria Brown and Mary Elliott had been responsible but numbers attending these meetings were not as large as they had been. The Sunday School remained sizable and there was an appeal for more teachers. When, in 1911, the day school moved out to occupy the newly-built council school on the other side of the Common there was talk of the Sunday School moving into the ex-school rooms but the teachers were not in favour so it did not happen until some years later[52].

Back in 1905, Church member John Gifford, with the encouragement of Alban Brown, had taken over as organist after Elton Thatcher resigned. Also in charge of the choir, in 1908 he supplemented it with boys and girls from the day school and took other steps that successfully improved the group's singing. The choir was formally thanked *'for the splendid efforts they had made to improve the devotional part of the church services'*. Later, at Lea's suggestion, 'Amen' was sung at the end of all hymns and a vesper hymn or verse sung by the choir at the close of the Sunday evening service.

Not all of Lea's idea were accepted as readily! The membership turned down his proposal to change the morning service from 10.45 to 11am as they did his plan for the church to have its own cemetery, on a site next to the new council school that he had already agreed with the local council.

---

[52] *The rooms behind the church were made available for use by 'sister churches' or by the village cricket club at no cost, although restrictions were put on the cricketers to protect the floor. Otherwise hire of the rooms for meetings not connected with the church was 2/6d, or 6/- if admission was being charged.*

Rev T G Vinson, chairman of the Worcestershire Congregational Union conducted several weeks of mission services towards the end of 1908 but Lea's proposal to repeat this two years later was turned down by the members. He was probably more successful with a suggestion to adopt a new hymn book, as this appears to have resulted in 'The Congregational Church Hymnal' being introduced.

When he asked a church meeting to approve his action in stopping dancing at the 1911 New Year choir social it was given after much debate. However, John Gifford then and there *'tendered his resignation of post of organist and membership of chapel and withdrew'*. Two deacons were appointed to induce him to reconsider - in which mission they were obviously successful as he remained organist for a quarter of a century.

Asked by the Bristol Congregational Union to *'form a new cause'* across at Bedminster, Lea and his wife Emily finished their ministry at Whiteshill, moving out of the Memorial Manse in September 1911. He served as pastor at West Street, Bedminster for eight years and then at churches in Long Ashton and Chepstow. In 1930 Lea, by then in his seventies, was asked to go as a 'special visitor' to advise on how to help churches in Jamaica that had suffered hurricane damage.

Stability in troubled times

At the second time of asking Rev George Jarvis accepted a call to the pastorate of the church, starting his ministry at  the beginning of 1912 - heralding a more settled time for the congregation even though Jarvis's two decades as pastor included the First World War and the early years, from the end of the 1920s, of the Great Depression.

He had turned down the pastorate for the first time when finishing his theological studies but now, a quarter of a century later, 'inherited' a church with barely half the membership of those earlier days. The 'official' number of members stood at 67, ten of whom he found had moved out of the district!

Rev George Jarvis

About 50 could typically be found at the monthly Communion service and Jarvis soon made regular attendance at this the measure of who counted as church members, and therefore entitled to vote at church business meetings. From 1916, attendees put a named ticket into the Communion offering bag so their participation could be recorded by the pastor – a practice encouraged by the Congregational Union in those days and which continued at Whiteshill for the next 60 years.

Some activities were continuing to thrive – in particular the Sunday School – and Jarvis encouraged ways of bringing in

The earliest known photograph of the chapel, dating back to at least the beginning of the 20th Century

not only adults but also young people, '*the backwardness of the young people in meeting with God's people*' starting to become apparent countywide. Open-air services were held on some Sunday nights and there is a record of Boys Brigade and Girls Brigade being formed.

In time for the centenary of the Sunday School in March 1914 (it having started up in Winterbourne two years before the church building was erected) the school rooms were renovated and the old day school desks and forms altered to better suit the needs of the Sunday School. Jarvis was keen to start a scout troop and backed the trial of a Saturday social club '*to keep the young people in the neighbourhood from going to Bristol*'.

But when it came to church services there was a limit to what Jarvis found acceptable in trying to engage with youngsters. On one occasion he objected to the idea of the Young Worshippers including a sketch in the programme for a special service - the minutes of the members' meeting at which he voiced his disapproval recording that '*there was much diversity of feeling*'.

Nevertheless during Jarvis's ministry there was growth in the number of young people within the church and two were on the overseas mission field by the time of his departure. Even during the final service at the close of his ministry, he had the pleasure of welcoming four young people into membership.

A strong feature of life at Whiteshill by this time, and for many decades to come, was Christian Endeavour[53] – the only week-day meetings (Junior and Senior) shown on the notice board outside the church.

Fred Harding, seen here in later life, set up Christian Endeavour at the chapel before World War One. His wife, Kate, was a founder of the Ladies Bright Hour in 1932.

Towards the beginning of Jarvis's ministry, the remaining few quarterly seat rent payments were dropped in favour of weekly envelopes and a few months later the letting of seats, the prime source of income for the chapel when it was founded a century earlier, finally came to an end with the removal of the notice in the church lobby offering seat rental.

Over the years, much renovation of the premises had to be carried out, in particular to the school rooms. With the day school having vacated the rooms, upkeep was no longer the responsibility of the local education authority. A fair proportion of the work was paid for by the pastor himself or carried out by builder Thomas Bridgeman Pendock, one

---

[53] *The first Christian Endeavour (CE) Society was founded in the United States in 1881. Its object was to bridge the gap between Sunday School and Church, bringing young people and young adults to Christ and preparing them for involvement in the activities of their church. In 1895 the British movement had one and a half million members and by 1900 there were over 6,000 CE Societies mainly attached to Baptist, Congregational and Primitive Methodist churches. CE holidays and conventions were where more than one Whiteshill youngster met their partner-to-be for the first time!*

of the deacons, at no cost to the church. A little later Fred (as he signed himself) Dove, who had taken over from his father as treasurer, contributed personally to help cover many of the church costs.

The church's centenary was celebrated in 1916 - half way through World War One - with special services on the last weekend of May and the first weekend of June. On the

A sunny day for the centenary tea

Wednesday in between, an outdoor tea for 200 people was followed by photographs being taken of the gathering before an evening service at which the three previous ministers, and the widow of the fourth (Mrs Eynon) each spoke.

The chapel children of the day join in the centenary celebrations with a special performance in the old school room.

Then the church closed its doors for several months while a new heating and ventilation system was installed;[54] the oil lamps replaced with acetylene gas lighting [55] - to be superseded by electric lighting in both church and manse 13 years later; and the organ taken to pieces to be

---

[54] *Thomas Bridgman Pendock supplied, for free, a second hand boiler and pipework. A contractor from Stapleton supplied and fitted the new heating system at a cost of £40 and two Boyle's Air Pump Extractors for £20. The pastor offered to pay the £60 if the church found the cost of fixing up the ventilating shafts and outlets.*

[55] *Acetylene gas is created by water dripping onto calcium carbide. The gas is then piped to light fixtures where it is burned, creating a very bright light. Occasionally at Whiteshill the acetylene gas lights would flicker and someone would have to go very quickly and re-establish the drip of water before the gas was all used up, plunging the chapel into darkness.*

thoroughly cleaned and tuned by the Bristol firm that had built it. Meanwhile the front lawn was raised with 40 loads of soil and then reseeded.

Mid-September saw services able to transfer back into the chapel (presumably from the schoolroom) and re-opening services were held, combined with Harvest Thanksgiving. It was agreed the time of the Sunday morning service would be moved forward 15 minutes to 11am - despite the fact this change had been ruled out not many years earlier!

The church in the late 1910s or in the 1920s, when it had gas lighting – overhead and at each end of the pulpit. In this period the choir pews were side on to the congregation, in front of the organ.

Only one person from the chapel is recorded as losing his life as a result of the First World War, however judging by the surnames of those listed on the parish war memorial it is more than likely some who attended the church lost family members or relatives in the conflict.

The one known death, of pneumonia while training for the war, was of Bert Roberts, *'our choicest young fellow … high in promise, gifted as an instrumentalist and most winsome as a lad and willing, loyal and consecrated as a young Christian'*. He was buried at Downend Cemetery with *'a goodly company'* walking there from Whiteshill.

As World War One came to an end *'Revival Services'* were conducted by William Olney from London, accompanied by a talented soloist Miss Minus. Hearts, as the pastor saw

it, were already softened by the loss of Roberts and others they knew who had died in the war. Over the 16 days of the mission, 33 children and 55 adults made *'the great decision'* and before long this led to a number of new people being added to the fellowship.

New Year's Day 1922 saw the unveiling of the parish War Memorial opposite the church, bearing the names of local men killed in the conflict. At the unveiling ceremony Jarvis and the rector of Winterbourne both spoke on the theme of 'Brotherhood'. Sadly, 25 years later more names had to be added.[56]

In 1919 the pastor advocated changing from a single cup to individual glasses for the wine at Communion services, leading several members to immediately offer to fund the purchase of three wooden Communion trays each holding 24 small glasses. These trays are still in use today, not far off a century later.

1919 Communion trays still in use today

The first to offer a contribution to the cost was Hambrook baker, Sydney Good, a trustee and a little later church secretary - and great grandson of chapel founding-father Nathaniel Good. Sydney's three daughters were active in the church, Gwendoline setting up and running a girl's club on a Friday evening *'rather than see them wandering'* and Irene, a trained nurse, serving in India as a medical missionary for many years from 1928 onwards.

Under the 20 year ministry of Jarvis numbers grew but not until well after the First World War. It became necessary to buy a fourth Communion tray in 1926 to increase the

---

[56] *In 1936 the British Legion pressed for the memorial to be fenced off to keep it 'more reverent' but local people successfully petitioned against any part of the Common being enclosed.*

number of Communion cups available from 72 to 96 and by the late 1920s there were over 100 names on the church roll and an average of 75 to 80 taking Communion.

Membership numbers stayed steady at around the 100 mark for the following five or six years although a decrease in those attending Communion might indicate that once again some people listed as members had in fact moved away or stopped attending for other reasons.

The view in the early 1920s looking left to Pye Corner from beyond the church gate.

An innovation of the inter-war period was annual *'Sportsmans Services'*. The local paper noted in 1923, *'A capital attendance of young Hambrook footballers and cricketers at the service, with their wives, sweethearts, mothers and sisters.'*

Jarvis had come to Whiteshill on a stipend of £100 a year (plus a rent free manse) which stayed the same for most of his years as pastor. By 1919 the Congregational Union was of the opinion that with inflation having spiked at 25% in 1917 and still at 15% after the war, no pastor could manage on less than £150 per annum and appealed to churches to contribute to a Church Aid fund to help poorly paid ministers.

Finances were not good at Whiteshill, but the members tried to heed the advice. Preferring not to look to the Union for help, they committed to make an effort to provide, one way or another, a bonus each year to supplement Jarvis's stipend.

This amounted to £50 for a couple of years but, as the economic effects of the country struggling to pay its war debts impacted on the whole population, and despite raising funds through organ recitals, choir concerts and sales of work, the best the church could manage was to have a special Easter offering to supplement, in some small measure, the pastor's income.

In the final years before Jarvis's retirement the chapel was able to increase his annual stipend to £120 – and dropped the idea of a bonus. Ironically, looking through the record books there was probably never a year when the pastor did not plough back into the church most, if not all, of what he was paid.

In July 1930 John Gifford retired[57], the pastor speaking of his *untiring work at the organ* when presenting him with an engraved gold watch at a social evening to mark his 25 years as the church organist. Gifford remarked how pleased he was that his son, Frank, was succeeding him. And Frank Gifford went on to double his father's record – occupying the organ stool for the next half century. Jack Miles agreed to become choir master and his son Dick, the deputy organist.

---

[57] *John Gifford died just over a year after retiring as organist, aged only 49.*

Frank Gifford (above) was organist for 50 years, following on from his father's 25 years.

The pastor's wife, Mary Rowles Jarvis, was an accomplished hymn writer, poet and author. Several of her compositions found their way into hymnals of the day including the 1916 'Congregational Hymnary', which was introduced at Whiteshill in the very year it was published. Many of her short stories and books for children were published. Mrs Jarvis passed on her interest in English literature to her daughter, Mary[58], who read the subject at Oxford University.

---

[58] *Jarvis's daughter, Mary Eveline Jarvis, having excelled in her studies at Monmouth High school, won a place at Oxford University where she passed the exams for a BA and MA degree in English language and literature, in 1914. This was several years before Oxford had started conferring degrees on women, so she had to wait until 1922 for it to be officially awarded. She went on to become headmistress of the Brecon Girl's County school and served as a magistrate.*

In 1931, his wife having died two years earlier, Jarvis decided it was time to retire that Easter, after nearly two decades at Whiteshill. He felt that, *'having passed my 70th year, I might reasonably ask for release'* but to the congregation the news *'came as a bombshell and … received it with much sorrow and regret'*.

Jarvis, in keeping with his quiet and unostentatious nature, had forbidden any retirement presentation from the church but the Sunday school *'by stealth'* succeeded in giving him a present of *'choice books and an inscribed umbrella'*.

The Jarvis family in the garden of the Memorial Manse

Temporary, part-time and short-lived pastorates

The church was in no rush for the pastor, Rev George Jarvis, to move out of the manse when he retired at the beginning of April 1931. It had been decided to fund a £100 renovation of the chapel while there was no stipend to pay to a minister and to rely on trainee ministers from the Congregational Union's Western College to conduct Sunday services with Bristol Itinerant Society preachers filling the pulpit on the second and third Sunday of each month.

By mid-year the work on the building had been completed by local builder and church deacon Harry Pendock and the church was officially re-opened by a member of the Wills family, with whom Whiteshill had retained strong links since its earliest days.

The following year a new meeting proved to be very popular and continued to be held for the next 75 years. Two of the church ladies – known to all as Mrs Willie Harding and Mrs Fred Harding (although sharing the same surname, not as far as is known related) – founded a weekly Ladies Bright Hour, in committee with Mrs S Good and Mrs J Gifford.

Intended as *'an oasis during the week for the ladies'*, the meeting included worship and a Bible message but was less formal than Sunday services - and included tea and biscuits half way through. Current church member Joy Lowe – who in much more recent years was Bright Hour President – recalls as a youngster going along with her mother and hearing the clicking of needles as more than a few got on with their knitting during the meeting!

The oldest known photograph of the Ladies Bright Hour. Taken in 1936, the ladies – teapot at the ready - enjoy a summer afternoon at Waterfall Farm, Moorend, home of the Churchill family.

Eight months after Jarvis's retirement, advertisements were placed in two Christian publications, seeking an experienced pastor to fill the Whiteshill vacancy – a break with earlier practice of selecting a new minister from amongst Western College students sent to preach at the church.

There was no shortage of suitable applicants but what the church learned was how fortunate it had been to have had a minister for the past 20 years who was prepared to accept a low salary! One after another potential minister turned out to be paid by their current church up to three times the sum Whiteshill felt able to offer.

While the search continued, at the suggestion of Western College, 25 years old Arthur Robert Down, originally from Exeter, agreed to become temporary pastor. He was already '*pledged*' to serve as a missionary in Madagascar with the London Missionary Society so could only be available for 12 months. Coming to Whiteshill in October 1932, true to his pledge, he left, with his wife Kathleen, to start his time as a missionary exactly one year later.[59]

A prime task for Down was to do what he could to help the church find a permanent minister.

Robert & Kathleen Down

However he did make some small changes to the services during his short ministry – dropping the singing of 'Amen' after the last hymn of each service and introducing a thanksgiving prayer after the offering.

Over the years the church had been involved in the activities of the Congregational Union Gloucester and Hereford District and paid an annual subscription to that organisation. However apart from a few years just before the First World War the church had never subscribed to the national body. During the 1920s and 30s the

---

[59] *Down was living in Madagascar when it became controlled by Vichy-France in World War Two. In 1942 the island was liberated in the first British amphibious assault of the war. The Bristol papers later reported that, 'Capt. Down rendered them great assistance as an interpreter and in other capacities. Mrs Down was the first white women to welcome the British troops …' Down served as an assistant Chaplain to the Forces on the island until 1946. He then pastored churches in the UK until retirement in the mid-1960s.*

Congregational Union of England and Wales had upon several occasions raised the matter with the church.

Despite being assured the chapel's independence would not be compromised by 'joining', the membership had formally voted against such a move when approached in 1926. However, during a visit from the Moderator in 1933, primarily to give advice on finding a new minister, the subject was once more raised. The result was a vote, narrowly in favour of joining, but the decision appears not to have been put into effect, as after this, annual subscriptions were still only paid to the District Union.

As it turned out, Whiteshill's next pastor, Bristol-born Donald Sinclair Simmons, was yet another man proposed by Western College – a Congregational Union organisation,

Rev Donald Simmons

incidentally, that the church did support year in and year out by way of a one guinea [£1/1/0] contribution.

Simmons was very different from the college's typical trainee ministers. He was a Cambridge University graduate, had become a senior master at Wellington College but now, in his late twenties, was embarking upon three years' study, three days a week at Western College, to complete ministerial training. Simmons had been a deacon and superintendent of the Sunday School at Wellington Congregational Church.

A recognition service for the new minister was held in October 1933 and although being in some respects a 'part-time' pastor, Simmons was nonetheless active and able in leading and organising the church over the next two-and-a-half years.

The membership agreed to a number of changes he proposed for the election of deacons – making the minimum age for deacons 21 years old and voting slips being issued to every member so they could all register a vote in the election of deacons, whether or not they attended the meeting at which the ballot was conducted. (For the next couple of decades there was change after change to the way deacons were elected, for how long they stayed in office, and how many deacons there should be.)

In what to some seemed a radical move, for the first time at Whiteshill, it was agreed women were to be eligible to stand for the office of deacon. However, records show no women becoming deacons and the decision was reversed on a very close vote, barely three years later, returning the church to only allowing an all-male diaconate. (To this day there have been no women deacons even though for some years the church rules have again made both men and women eligible.)

Simmons was keen to encourage young people, holding special young people's services on the last Sunday evening of each month. For these services the gallery, which had been out of use for some time, was re-opened. Improvements to the bookrests in front of the choir seats were agreed but a proposal to have raised bookrests and tiered choir seats was turned down by the church membership.

The organ was professionally cleaned, retuned and a second-hand tremulant[60] fitted, but there was much debate, as there had been for some long time, about whether or not it was appropriate for a piano to be used in the church. Those who felt that only the organ was suitable for use in church held sway but eventually it was agreed that with sufficient and proper notice a piano could be permitted in the church for special occasions involving the children!

It might have been the 'thin end of the wedge' but it was not until the late 1940s that a piano was permanently positioned in the church, initially on the other side of the pulpit from the organ.

By 1935 the rise of militarism in Europe was a concern and along with many churches, the Whiteshill congregation felt it their Christian duty to call for peace among nations. A prayer for peace was pasted into each hymn book and the following year there was support for the Bristol Peace Council with some of the congregation attending demonstrations against rearmament.

His studies in Bristol coming to an end and having accepted a call to a pastorate in Stratford-on-Avon, [61] Simmons proposed that the church consider uniting with another

---

[60] *A tremulant is a device on a pipe organ which varies the wind supply to the pipes of one or more divisions. This causes their amplitude and pitch to fluctuate, producing a tremolo and vibrato effect.*

[61] *After 30 years as pastor of churches in Stratford-upon-Avon, Rugby and Highgate in Middlesex, Simmons was appointed assistant Home Secretary of the London Missionary Society. In 1966, moving towards combining with the Presbyterian Church to become the United Reform Church (URC), the Congregational Union re-organised itself into the Congregational Church in England and Wales with Simmons as assistant Secretary. The URC came into being in 1972 and Simmons, by then in his late sixties, took on part-time pastorates of two churches in Devon.*

Congregational church - either Frampton Cotterell (now Zion United church) or Morley Memorial church (in Lodge Causeway, Fishponds). As an alternative, he suggested seeking Rev David Roberts as pastor, whom he knew was about to give up the pastorate of Clifton Down Congregational church.

Keen to continue to have their own pastor, a pulpit swap was speedily arranged so the congregation could meet Roberts and hear him preach – after which the church took no time at all in asking him to accept the pastorate, which he did from January 1937.

Rev David John Roberts

Following on from one temporary and one part-time minister it was expected that Roberts, already one of Bristol's best known Congregational ministers, [62] would use his renowned energy and organisational skills along with his strength in preaching and teaching to make his mark on Whiteshill for a good long period of time.

As with several new pastors, one of Roberts' early tasks was to delete from the membership roll a dozen or so names of those who had either moved away or, despite having been

[62] *After pastoring churches in his native Wales, Roberts was minister, for 16 years, of Bristol's Castle Green Congregational church in Greenbank Road, Eastville (the 1901-built successor to Castle Green church in central Bristol from where the Whiteshill pulpit came in 1816) before moving to Clifton Down Congregational church. He was secretary of the Bristol Congregational Union.*

visited, no longer wanted to attend the church. Clearly the size of the congregation had drifted downwards considerably over the previous few years; the lower numbers attending services making the use of the balcony unnecessary.

Widowed before he arrived at Whiteshill, but ably assisted by his unmarried daughter, Roberts soon put together his ideas for a series of monthly *'special efforts'*, more publicity of church services and events, and a *'visiting campaign'* to address this downward trend.

His daughter began planning concerts and *'musical services'* with guest choirs and soloists from other churches for the Sunday afternoon of the church anniversary and for the harvest weekend to be held in September. And, not a new idea for Whiteshill, there was a special Easter offering to bolster the poor state of church funds.

With church life just beginning to step up a gear, barely seven months after his recognition service at Whiteshill, on 25th August 1937 Roberts died suddenly at the manse, leaving the church once again without a pastor.

Living through another war

After the totally unexpected death of Rev David Roberts, it was realised that finding a new pastor would take time so there was no problem in inviting his daughter to continue to live at the manse *'for as long as she required'*.

In fact, she moved back into Bristol six months after her father's death, transferring membership to Highbury Congregational church in March 1938. Before her move, she presented a brass vase to the church, inscribed in memory of her father; it still being put to good use upon occasion for the church flowers.

Much in favour of the programme the late pastor had mapped out, the members went ahead with the *'special efforts'* he had 'pencilled in' for the rest of the year. Roberts' son[63], himself a minister, agreed to take his father's place in conducting all three of the harvest services (the fruit and vegetables, as usual, being shared between the village hospital and the Bristol Royal Infirmary). From the beginning of the next year, due to insufficient numbers by then attending, the concerts and suppers were put on hold.

By February 1938, with no suitable replacement pastor in sight from the applications received or names suggested, the deacons started to explore the possibility of a link-up with the Congregational church in Frampton Cotterell, *'so that we could have a younger qualified minister'*. This statement

---

[63] *Whiteshill pastor David John Roberts' son – whose name was David Trevor Roberts - followed in his father's footsteps by training at Western College to become a Congregational minister. He led a number of churches in Yorkshire and in the mid-1950s became chairman of that county's Congregational Union.*

might say something about the age and level of training of those who had applied for the pastorate – and the 'quality' of the man the church could expect as pastor for the salary that could be afforded!

Then, came a letter from a friend of the church, suggesting the deacons approach a man from Bexley in Kent; Rev George Henry Clothier – who was looking to move to the Bristol area. This they did and after he came to preach, almost a year to the day after the previous incumbent had died, Clothier was asked to become Whiteshill's next pastor.

Within the space of only a couple of months, the Clothiers – George and his wife Mary - had moved into the manse (that had been rapidly re-decorated by volunteers ready for their arrival) and George Clothier was formally inducted into the pastorate in October 1938.

Clothier did not come from the same mould as Whiteshill pastors of earlier times; his background was less 'moneyed' and he was 'a local', unlike most of the earlier ministers. One important common factor he did share with the majority of Whiteshill ministers was the college where he gained his theological training.

He was the son of a Bedminster police constable and reaching his 15th birthday in 1890, embarked upon an apprenticeship in Great Western Railway's Bristol Goods department. After six years he left to begin theological training at the Congregational Union Western College which, during this period, was in Plymouth.

Having completed training he spent the next 40 years as a minister, first in the West Country, then in the Home Counties. Seeing retirement not too far away, Clothier was keen to spend a few years back in his 'native heath', having been born in Bristol. At 63 years old when he came to the church, he was not the young pastor Whiteshill ideally had in mind, but having met him and heard him preach, the members were unanimous in deciding he was the right man for the church.

Compared to the short time each of the previous three ministers had filled the role of Whiteshill pastor, Clothier brought a slightly greater degree of stability, remaining as pastor for five-and-a-half years.

Church life was flagging, with numbers continuing to drop at the time Clothier arrived and he sought to breathe into it some renewed vigour. He reinstated the week-night prayer and fellowship meetings; introduced, after the evening service on one Sunday a month a short prayer meeting and, after another, a young people's meeting. Although thought inadvisable and unnecessary in light of the reduced numbers attending, the pastor re-opened the balcony for some Sunday evening services as that was where the young people preferred to sit.

After some discussion it was agreed to set up a week-night social club for young men, the committee for which almost straight away asked and gained permission for the 'Whiteshill Congregational Social Club' to include young ladies as well. But another request from the club was unanimously refused – the use of playing cards!

Monthly open air services were held on the Common, opposite the church, during the Summer of 1939 and a fete held that July was declared a success when there were 52 entries for the Best Cake competition! Lantern slide lectures were conducted (one on the Life and Times of Martin Luther) and films were projected for the social club. Renewed church activity was soon curtailed when, within 12 months of Clothier's arrival, Britain was again at war.

Unlike the First World War, when church life was not too directly affected by the conflict, this time an increasing number of the congregation was called-up each year. The upper age limit for conscription increased from 22 to 41 and then by 1942 covered men up to age 51 and unmarried women between 20 and 30 years old. In time, 25 people attending a Communion service became a high number!

The Sunday School and the Ladies Bright Hour continued to be well supported – it being mainly the men who had to leave for the war. (The Ladies Bright Hour was probably the first organisation at the church to use electricity for more than lighting when in 1942 they connected in – in place of a light bulb - an electric ring to boil water for cups of tea, as it was impossible to get their primus stove repaired due to the war.)

An example of the difficulties encountered in church life was when church member Dick Miles accepted the position of choirmaster (made vacant by church secretary and deacon H W Harrison) as well as already being assistant organist, only to resign both jobs within days, his call-up papers having dropped through the letterbox. Numbers at services became very low, sometimes boosted a little on Sunday mornings by soldiers from the nearby Conifers and Cross Road military camps.

An *active service wallet*, holding a copy of St Mark's Gospel plus prayers and hymns, was sent to all those connected with the church who were called-up. In conjunction with the British Legion, the congregation gave donations each year so that a Christmas gift could go to each man associated with the local churches who was serving in the forces; 5/- for those on active service and 2/6d to the others.

A *prayer list* giving the name of *each man and girl* from the Whiteshill congregation who were in the forces or away on other war work was put up in the church foyer, with extra names having to be added as the war progressed.

Due to the number who were absent, because of wartime restrictions and shortages, or due to the threat of bombing, most week-night activities and special events had to stop for at least part of the war. In winter the 6pm service was brought forward to 3.15pm [64] to comply with blackout regulations and for a while it is possible only a morning service was held.

Even the church magazine was affected when bombing destroyed the Bristol printing works of church member, and later treasurer, Philip Dove, where it was being produced. In November 1940, returning home with her father after a 3.15pm Sunday service, church member June Collett (nee Gifford) vividly remembers rushing for shelter when enemy planes flew low overhead. Looking towards Bristol the red sky they saw signalled the first night of the Bristol Blitz.

The old school rooms at the back of the church were designated as a Rest Centre where on a number of occasions families whose homes had been bombed were given emergency overnight shelter. Clothier was 'Marshalman' for the Centre as well as being the official chaplain to the four armed forces camps in the neighbourhood and to wounded British soldiers in the Frenchay American hospital. He sometimes took services at Frenchay church for American soldiers based locally.

---

[64] *Long-time member of the congregation Geoff Hibbard recalls, as a youngster, being paid 3d a time to pump the organ for these wartime afternoon services, with Pax Underwood (whose initials can be seen carved on the wooden panel at the back of the organ!) pumping it for the morning services.*

The church expected to lose the chapel gates as, throughout the country, metal gates and railings were removed to be used in producing military equipment. But, to the surprise of the deacons, a letter arrived from the relevant authority to say the gates, dating back to the building of the chapel in 1816, would not be taken.

During the war years it proved impossible to employ a caretaker, as had been done up until that time. This was in spite of being able to offer an increased payment for the job when the local education authority agreed a grant towards the cost, in the light of the church running a youth club. A rota of volunteer ladies to clean, and a man to see to the heating apparatus, had to be arranged and it was not until the end of the war that the paid position could be filled.

Later on in the war, with the reduced threat of bombing, the club for young people expanded to occupy both the upstairs and the downstairs school room, usually being open three nights a week (Tuesday, Thursday and Saturday) – with boys and girls meeting separately. After some debate it was agreed that boys over the age of 16 could smoke at the club.

At the end of 1943, now 68 years old, Clothier decided it was time to retire and return, with his wife Mary, to Bexley in Kent, where their daughter lived. Seeking a new pastor, the church was highly impressed with the preaching of an elderly minister from Taunton, but decided that a younger man would be more suitable when they took into account the younger members of the congregation – many of whom were away in the armed forces.

For the only time in its history, the church looked to a lay minister, Rev John Davies[65], who served the church for the next two years, beginning in October 1944. Davies, for the previous five years lay minister of Kingsland Congregational church in the St Philips area of Bristol, came to Whiteshill while continuing his 'day-time' employment with the Bristol Evening Post.

The church had in mind that Davies would, in due course, give up secular employment and become full-time pastor but it appears that he remained 'part-time' for the whole of his stay at Whiteshill.

On the church letterhead Davis's name carried the initials 'OCF' after it. 'CF' being the official abbreviation for 'Chaplain to the Forces' he might have also fulfilled some role of this sort, although if that was the case it is not clear for what the 'O' stood.

When Davies, and his wife Mary, moved on from Whiteshill[66] in the latter part of 1946 the church was able to call on the previous minister, Rev George Clothier, to help

---

[65] *Davies was classified as a lay minister by the Congregational Union although ordained, because he held a secular job alongside being a minister. Other Whiteshill pastors (Simmons for instance) studied for the ministry alongside serving the church at Whiteshill.*

[66] *After John and Mary Davies left there was a fear that the unoccupied manse would be requisitioned to house people whose homes had been destroyed in the war-time bombing. The County Council's view was that they would be able to requisition the house but deacon Tom Crang contacted the Ministry of Health who ruled that this was not the case.*

Rev George & Mrs Helena Clothier

out, as he had returned to the district, and to the church, after the death two years earlier of his wife, Mary.

Clothier willingly conducted many of the Sunday services and became an active member of the church, but without taking on the role of pastor again. Cementing his renewed link with the church, in April 1946 Clothier had married Mrs Helena Mann,[67] a widow who, having transferred to the church at Whiteshill in 1935 from Winterbourne Down was heavily involved in the work of the church. Among other responsibilities she led the Sunday School and children's activities in the war years.

During the war, the number of members able to attend church regularly at Whiteshill had reduced year by year to a total of little more than 30 men and women; the number called up or away due to the war increasing to around 20. After the cessation of hostilities in 1945 numbers increased

---

[67] *Clothier and his second wife, Helena (known to Whiteshill as Ellen), lived near the church, at The Sturdons in Quarry Barton. They remained church members until George Clothier died (at Frenchay Hospital) in July 1951 and Helena in May 1964.*

but with the death of some older members and others leaving the district, attendance only rose to around 40.

Longest-serving minister

Seeking a new minister to lead the church out of the low point in which it found itself immediately after the Second World War, the congregation looked both within the Congregational Union and elsewhere for the right person. The recommendation from the Union Moderator was Mrs Edith Seaton, an Oxford University graduate looking to move on from a period as minister of a church in London[68].

At a time when the church did not even permit women deacons, it seems strange that a woman minister would be considered, but nevertheless she was invited to preach at the church anniversary and there is nothing in the deacons' or the members' meeting minutes to suggest anyone voicing objections to the principle of calling a women as pastor.

However, a few weeks earlier, the speaker at the Whiteshill Christian Endeavour anniversary had been Alec Hutchings from the Bristol City Mission, invited after he had mentioned to one of the deacons that he would be prepared to consider the Whiteshill pastorate if asked.

Both the deacons and the church members were unanimous in deciding that Hutchings, aged in his forties, was the right person for Whiteshill – and he went on to become the

---

[68] *The Congregational Union is credited with being the earliest 'mainstream' Christian denomination to ordain women. Constance Coltman was the first, ordained in 1917 after obtaining a Bachelor of Divinity degree at Mansfield College, Oxford, having previously read History in Somerville College, Oxford.*

longest serving pastor the church has ever had - 28 years ministry by the time he retired at the close of 1975.

On a Wednesday in May 1947 a crowded church witnessed the induction of Alexander George Hutchings into the Whiteshill pastorate and with his wife Ivy, daughter Mary plus Rose Williams, who lived with the family, was soon settled in at the Memorial Manse. (Three years later, 27 years-old Mary married Eric Bryant who was for many years Whiteshill church secretary from the mid-1950s.)

After the restrictions of the war years a wide range of church activities - and congregation numbers - began to grow and flourish under the spiritual and practical care of the new and enthusiastic pastor. By the early 1950s numbers had doubled and stayed fairly steady for most of the next two decades. (Among new church members in 1948 was a young ex-prisoner of war Franz – known as Francis - Wondrak who stayed on locally after his release and three years later married Sheila Edwards, also a church member.)

The practice of holding open-air meetings on the Common across from the church in the summer months was re-started. Maybe due to the increased numbers involved or possibly with the village by these times identifying less with the chapel, there were local complaints. For the first time the church was forced to seek official permission from the parish council to hold these meetings.

Seemingly a common theme for new pastors at Whiteshill, the church roll had to be thoroughly reviewed when Hutchings began his ministry as it contained many names of people who never attended – and a few who were no longer alive! Letters and a reply card were sent to every name on the roll for them to confirm their *fellowship*.

Nevertheless 'real' membership was growing and it was decided to provide, each year, a list of the men of the church from which members could vote for the seven they felt most suitable to be church deacons; these seven being in addition to two who had by this time been elected as 'life-deacons'.

Pastor and deacons in 1950. Left to right; [back row] Thomas Crang, Herbert Harding, Frederick Lewis, Philip Dove, Douglas Fitz, Edward Hollyman, [front row] Christopher H Churchill, Francis G Whatley, pastor Alec Hutchings, Frederick C Harding, William Shean. Churchill, Whatley and F C Harding were 'life deacons'.

A Fabric Fund was set up to provide for modernisation of the premises. An active man in all respects, Hutchings organised, and himself carried out, many of the changes to the building that were needed to bring it up-to-date and to better suit the needs of the day.

As was general across the country, more use was soon being made of electricity, with a hearing aid loop being introduced and a water boiler being installed. By 1948 there was no longer a job for an *'organ boy'*, an electric motor having done away with the need to pay £1/10/0 a year to have the organ hand-pumped. Some electric fires were installed but the need for coal and coke did not come to an end until the installation of an oil-fired boiler heating system over 20 years later.

Financial giving improved to the point where the church funds were too great to continue being held in cash by the treasurer at his home, so the church's first bank account was opened. A *'gratifying balance'* of £37/11/2¾ could be reported at the start of 1949, and in the same year, a special Easter offering raised the considerable sum of £256 for redecorating the church, along with another £122 promised by way of interest free loans.

Hutchings encouraged musical and singing talent and one of his early initiatives was to have an area alongside the pulpit built up to permanently accommodate a piano. The mixed church choir increased in number and there was talk of repositioning the organ (possibly into the balcony, as had been suggested many decades earlier) to provide more space for the choir.

An alternative plan, carried out while the main church was out of use for redecoration, moved the choir seats from in front of the organ to the other side of the church. Pews displaced by moving the choir stools were fitted in the balcony.

Two new doorways were knocked through from the church; one to the school room[69] to give easy access to the

---

[69] *This new doorway was knocked through the back of what had until then been a china cupboard in the old school room. It therefore seems likely that there had*

re-positioned choir stools and the other under a side window leading to what became in due course a new vestry. The old side door to the vestry was blocked off, later providing a china cupboard in the wall cavity, in what became a kitchen. (Part of that cavity now houses a radiator in the main church).

With the changes complete and the church back in use by the end of August 1949, the text, 'O worship the Lord in the beauty of holiness', from Psalm 96, was sign-written on the wall above the pulpit. Chosen by the congregation from a number of suggestions, this particular Bible verse was proposed by life-deacon Francis Whatley.

As well as the pastor making alterations over the years to provide separate vestry, kitchen and toilet within the structure on the side of the church, in 1957 with the help of other men, the upstairs room was divided into two and a second staircase built from the ground floor.

Both before the war and afterwards there were strong links with the local cricket club which played on the Common across the road from the church. Players were allowed to use the toilets, the top landing (but not the top room) for changing, and later, for a small fee, the electric boiler.

But in 1952 they were asked to find other accommodation as their boot studs *were not helping the condition of the staircase and landing*. Even if they actually stopped using the landing at that time, it appears they continued to be allowed to use the toilets and in 1954 the church lobbied the

---

previously been a doorway that had been blocked up in earlier times, most likely when the schoolrooms were added onto the back of the chapel, and the resulting wall cavity used as a cupboard.

How has the building changed since this snowy day in the winter of 1954? The most noticeable difference is that an electric lamp on a wrought iron arch now sits atop the front gates – added around the end of the 1950s. In 1966 the front wall was made lower than it is in this picture and 1974 saw the ventilator housing on the roof done away with when the church was re-roofed.

local council on their behalf to provide toilets on the Common.

For many years the prize-winning Hambrook Silver Band practised in one of the old school rooms once a week and had their own small storeroom to house the instruments. Jack Miles and then his son, Dick – both heavily involved with music and choir at the church – were conductors of the band.

In 1964 the Band moved across to the new pavilion on the Common where they could practice more than once a week. For a few years after the war, local council meetings were also held in the school room. Smoking in the premises continued to be thought a 'delicate matter' so no action was taken on the issue.

A changing scene

The state of the Memorial manse had been an issue from when Alec Hutchings and his family first occupied it on their arrival in 1947. It was redecorated, mostly by the pastor himself, but the poor condition of the building could not be disguised by a layer of paint. There was considerable woodworm and a damp crumbling floor, not helped by the building lacking a damp course. At the beginning of the 1950s it was decided a new manse was needed.

The hope was that local builder Simmonds – whose family links went back to the very start of the church and whose yard was right next to the Memorial manse - would build a new manse on another plot and take the old one in payment. The thinking was that he would have the expertise to then structurally renovate and sell the 'old' manse. While to the church this seemed a good idea, unfortunately, it did not make business sense to Simmonds!

Not to be put off, the church looked around for a local site to buy, on which a new manse could be built. After the church rejecting one potential site as unsuitable, deacon Bert Harding offered to sell a plot of land fronting onto the Old Gloucester Road in Hambrook – part of the land he used for his market garden business. The offer gladly accepted, a building licence was granted in 1951 and the following year a quote of £2,500 accepted from another local builder, Maggs, to construct a four bedroom house.

On 30th October 1952 the house was dedicated to the Lord's work; it was built but there was still much to be done by volunteers over several years to finish everything off. For instance, it was only in 1957 that the money was found to run a water main into the house.

The Congregational Union had proposed a loan to cover the full cost of putting up the building but the membership preferred not to take up the offer. Selling the old manse did not turn out to be easy and its value proved insufficient to cover the building of the new one. The congregation gave generously and worked hard to raise funds but a gradually reducing debt remained on the books for quite a few years. Hutchings even offered to take on 'secondary employment' to help the financial situation if the congregation wanted.

Building and paying for the new manse did not distract from a full and varied church life of worship, teaching and Christian fellowship. Sunday School, Bible Class, Ladies Bright Hour, Christian Endeavour (Junior and Senior), Young People's Fellowship, choirs; these were just some of the activities beyond weekly prayer meetings and Sunday services, the latter often rounded off with an informal time of song and testimony after the evening worship.

Quite a number of people used the buses to get to meetings and in the late 1950s Hutchings contacted the Bristol Omnibus Company to point out the inconvenience of the bus leaving the centre of Bristol on Sundays at 5.40pm not reaching the chapel until nine minutes after the evening service had begun. The bus company readily agreed to alter the timetable the next time it was printed, so that the bus would arrive just before 6pm. What a different world it was 60 years ago!

Whiteshill's Christian Endeavour involvement stretched beyond the local church when member Mrs Doris Crang[70] held annual office as President of the West of England Christian Endeavour Federation in 1958/1959, in addition to already being the Junior Convener.

Doris Crang, wearing the CE regional president's chain of office

Under her leadership, the 1959 Easter Convention of some 800 'Endeavourers' was held in Bristol with meetings centred on Whiteshill and Horfield Baptist church. One hundred of the young people attending the convention were accommodated for the weekend at Hambrook primary school, on the opposite side of the Common from the church.

Christian Endeavour (CE) was still flourishing at Whiteshill but overall, across the country, numbers were dropping. In

---

[70] *Doris Irene Crang was known to most as 'Poppy'. Her father, Fred (Frederick Charles) Harding, had started both Junior and Senior Christian Endeavour Societies at Whiteshill before the First World War. As a young child Poppy was taken with her father, by pony and trap, to CE meetings at the church, where she was allowed to go to sleep sitting in the school room desks! Thus began a lifetime interest in CE; taking over leadership of Whiteshill Junior CE at age 16 and at a CE holiday at Weston-super-Mare meeting Tom Crang who became her husband in 1931. Their daughters, Lorna and Joan followed into leadership within CE at the church. Poppy's mother, Kate Emeline Harding, was one of two unrelated Mrs Hardings who were founders of the Whiteshill Ladies Bright Hour in 1932.*

1958 there were 184 CE Societies (or groups) in the West of England and Mrs Crang had a busy year visiting ten or more different CE anniversaries or local conventions each month.

Membership in the region stood at nearly 2,900 although in her annual report as president, Mrs Crang voiced her concern that over the previous five years that number had dropped by 900. Young children were not coming into CE as they had in the past – a sign of the times which was equally manifest in declining Sunday School numbers.

In November 1965, to progress talks on uniting with the Presbyterian church of England (to form the United Reform Church) all Congregational churches were asked to 'covenant' together to form a single body. Having always valued its independence, and in light of the Congregational Union having by this time moved away from the conservative evangelical position held by Whiteshill the deacons unanimously recommended, and the church members agreed, not to enter into this covenant.

Thus, any formal link with the Congregational Union was broken. Despite the Union national moderator, Dr Coggan – who had already been invited to speak at Whiteshill's 150th anniversary services the following year – proposing further discussion on the subject, it was decided '*that the matter had been fully dealt with*'.

In the order of 2,000 Congregational churches agreed to the covenant but another 700 followed the same path as Whiteshill, a number then affiliating with the FIEC (Fellowship of Independent Evangelical Churches) and others with the smaller Congregational Federation or EFCC (Evangelical Fellowship of Congregational Churches). Although immediately invited to become affiliated with the

FIEC, Whiteshill did not take that step until more than a decade later.

Even before ending its link with the Congregational Union the possibility of believers' baptism by total immersion for those who profess belief in Christ as their Saviour, rather than the Congregational practice of infant baptism, was being voiced by church members. As time went on, a number of church young people asked for believers' baptism and these were conducted by 'borrowing' other churches which had a baptismal pool.

Feeling freer to support missionary activity beyond that of the Congregational Union's London Missionary Society, towards the end of 1966 the church formed a missionary committee. The following year it was decided that five percent of each week's offerings should be devoted to support of missionaries in which the church had an interest. This practice continues today, but now with ten percent of weekly offerings – no longer collected by passing offering bags around the congregation - being put to this use.

The morning service each Sunday was beginning to replace the evening worship as the better attended meeting[71] and it was decided to conduct Communion during a morning service four times a year. This was in addition to once a month at an evening service which had been the practice of the church. Several years later it was decided to include Communion in both a morning and an evening service each month and this has happened ever since.

---

[71] *In 1968 at a members' meeting, the pastor expressed his concern that only 60 people had attended the Sunday evening service in the previous few weeks.*

In no way replacing the mixed church choir, in 1972 a 22-strong male voice choir was formed under the conductorship of Doug Fitz, furthering the church's strong musical tradition. The choirmen undertook 'gospel' singing engagements for several decades at other churches as well as taking part in services at Whiteshill.

Today the church does not have its own choir, but several of the same men are still involved in gospel singing, with the Bristol Evangel Male Voice Choir which practices at Whiteshill each week under the direction of Paul Davies and as part of the Bristol and West of England Festivals of Male Voice Praise. (Also these days, on another evening of the week the church is home to a sizeable group of men and women singers, who make up the Emmaus Christian Choir.)

Although he stayed on as a church and choir member for a time afterwards, the retirement of pastor Hutchings, whose wife, Ivy, had died two years earlier, was formally marked on the very last day of 1975. Each of the many church organisations Hutchings had nurtured over 28 years as minister participated in word or song including the Bible Class, Sunday School, Young Worshippers, Christian Endeavour, Young People's Fellowship, Ladies Bright Hour, Church and Male Voice choirs … and others.

Bringing the story up to date

With a replacement minister needed after the retirement of Alec Hutchings the membership this time looked beyond the Congregational Union. After two years of visiting speakers Rev Barry Blake-Lobb, who had been with a church in Northern Ireland, was invited to become pastor of what had seven years previously been renamed Whiteshill Evangelical Church.

During his two years at Whiteshill, from 1977 to 1979, a written Basis of Faith, constitution and church rules were formulated and agreed. It was a time of change for the church as it sought God's way forward having moved away from its Congregational roots and after the best part of 30 years led by one pastor. While most stayed at Whiteshill some members decided to worship elsewhere, either permanently or for a period of time. Over time new people arrived and felt comfortable with the direction in which the church was travelling.

For some time the numbers of children and young people had continued to decrease and changes were made, introducing 'Covie' and 'Juco' groups for the older children and a new style Sunday School was renamed 'Adventurers'. All the groups changed to meeting on a Sunday morning instead of in the afternoon. As happens now, they joined in the first part of the Sunday morning worship service before going to their own sessions. The older groups also met for social activities on one night a week.

After Blake-Lobb moved on to work with the Billy Graham organisation in Australia the Rev Eric Newman was called to be minister. He commenced in 1980, following 20 years as minister of Calne Free Church, in Wiltshire. Soon after

Rev Eric and Mrs Newman

his induction at Whiteshill in March 1981, the go ahead was given for a baptistry to be constructed at the front of the church and the first adult baptisms by total immersion were on Whit Sunday 1982.

The result of an approach from a church neighbour, land to the side of the church was bought and initially

Single-storey building extension takes shape in the late 1980s

'opened up' for car parking while a side extension was designed and agreed with South Gloucestershire Council planners. Work on the extension (providing a new entrance, toilets, side room, kitchen and boiler room) was not completed until the next pastor, Rev Daryl Jones was in place but Newman was invited back to perform the official ribbon-cutting opening in March 1991.

After a degree in civil engineering and a time employed by West Sussex county council, Daryl had worked with UCCF (Universities and Colleges Christian Fellowship) for five years as a travelling secretary in the London area. During the eight years Daryl and his wife Julia were at Whiteshill various work was done on other parts of the church building. A music group was formed to accompany singing at services and Mission Praise hymn books were increasingly used in addition to the existing Congregational Praise books.

Rev Daryl & Mrs Julia Jones

When Daryl, Julia – and by then their two children - moved on to Limes Avenue Baptist Church in Aylesbury in 1998 there was a couple of years without a pastor until Rev Martin Moore, with his wife Joy, came to Whiteshill having undertaken theological training at Moorlands Bible College in Bournemouth.

Halfway through Martin's ten year ministry there was another change of manse. The somewhat isolated manse in Hambrook was sold in favour of a more modern house in Bradley Stoke in 2005. Mirroring their predecessors, Martin and Joy had two children during their decade at Whiteshill. The family of four bade farewell to Whiteshill in the summer of 2010 for Richmond Park Church in Boscombe, not many miles from the college at which Martin had trained.

The next – and current - Whiteshill pastor, Rev David Horton arrived at Easter 2013. Both David and his wife Hazel trained at Moorlands Bible College before spending ten years working with Africa Inland Mission in Madagascar.

Down through the years various editions of the Mission Praise hymn book had been used, for a time alongside Congregational Praise. New songs began to be introduced, thrown up onto a large screen using an Overhead Projector. In time superseded by a computer-driven projector, that technology has now been replaced by a large computer monitor onto which the mixture of traditional and modern worship songs used at services is shown – as well as Bible readings and notices.

The pipe organ still accompanies the singing of traditional hymns, while piano, keyboard and guitars fit better with the newer worship songs. Alongside this band of instrumentalists, two or three singers lead the congregational singing. Numbers attending Whiteshill Sunday services appear to be slowly on the increase but, apart from on special occasions, are a far cry from generations ago – 70 in the morning is not unknown but closer to half that number is typical for evening worship.

Keen to engage with the local community, special events are organised throughout the year and these are well supported. Most popular is the carol-singing and barbecue held in the church grounds and attracting 200 people or more – an opportunity the church values to tell out the real message of Christmas between singing well-loved traditional carols.

The first six months of the church 200th anniversary year – 2016 - saw pastor David Horton conducting the services in the old downstairs school room while the most extensive renovation the main 'chapel' had ever seen, took place.

David – current minister - and Hazel Horton

For some time consideration had been given to renovating the church but it became necessary to do something without delay when a professional inspection of the church ceiling, hidden from view for several decades by a suspended tile ceiling, not only found it beyond repair but more worryingly could not say whether or not parts of it were likely to fall down any time soon!

It was decided to seek listed building consent for a whole programme of work. That permission granted, the main worship area became out of bounds to allow specialist contractors to replace the entire ceiling – a very time-consuming (and expensive) process as it had to be carried out using the very same lath and lime plaster technique employed when the building was erected in 1816.

In parallel with replacing the ceiling, a completely new, more efficient, heating system was installed throughout the building, LED lighting put in, electrics updated, the toilets refurbished and reconfigured to provide a dedicated disabled toilet and baby-changing facility, and new double-glazed roof lights fitted in the school room. The outside and most of the interior of the building was then redecorated and a few months later the kitchen re-equipped, primarily to provide more potential for cooking meals occasionally.

Even before the scaffolding could be erected to get to the church ceiling, the supports holding up the church floor had to be repaired to make the floor level and able to support the weight of the scaffolding. Levelling the floor had the added benefit of returning the pipe organ to its original vertical position, the top of it having gently leant against the church side wall for decades!

Not unexpectedly in view of the age of the building, as the scheduled work progressed, other problems were unearthed and had to be dealt with. The biggest extra job that arose was fitting new ironwork across the ceiling of the upstairs old schoolroom to prevent the possibility of its outer wall leaning outwards at an even greater angle than it had for as long as anyone could remember!

But everything was completed well in time to accommodate a near-full church on Sunday 28th August – 200 years to the

very date that the chapel had first opened. The Bishop of Bristol, Rt Revd Mike Hill was the guest speaker – by co-incidence the same surname as the preacher at the opening of the chapel two centuries earlier.

A special morning service, led by current pastor David Horton, with the two previous ministers, Martin Moore and Daryl Jones also taking part, culminated in the unveiling, by the bishop, of a commemorative plaque in the foyer.

The Bishop of Bristol (left) unveiled the 200th anniversary plaque in the church foyer.

In lovely sunshine around 120 of the congregation stayed on for lunch in marquees on the lawn, most spending the afternoon sharing memories, looking at the specially produced floral arrangements, art exhibition and history exhibits around the church, or for those who wanted some exercise, joining a guided heritage walk linking places in the village with the chapel's early history.

A celebratory Songs of Praise was held later in the afternoon, rounded off by the cutting - and eating - of a commemorative cake made and intricately decorated by church member Anne Lloyd.

The following day, Bank holiday Monday, saw large numbers of local people take up the invitation to look round the church, then sit outside listening to everything from a ukulele band to jazz musicians and enjoy a cream tea while the youngsters took part in games spread around the grounds. A short organ recital was given during the afternoon – the first opportunity to witness the noticeable improvement the new ceiling gives to the acoustics of the church.

Throughout a year of celebratory events marking 200 years of unbroken worship and proclamation of the good news of Jesus Christ, the outside of the building was draped with a large banner. It noted the special year for the church with these Bible words from Hebrews chapter 13 verse 8: 'Jesus Christ, the same yesterday, today and forever'.

The church in 2016, displaying its 200th anniversary banner

As this account of the history of the church illustrates, much has changed both within the walls of the chapel and within society, over the course of 200 years. But what today's congregation believes - as did those first worshippers two centuries ago - is that God's love and offer of salvation through the Lord Jesus Christ is unchanged from generation to generation.

Minister	Whiteshill Ministry
Samuel WESTON	1822 - 1832
W ELLSON	1833 - 1835
John AVERILL	1839 - 1845
Charles KNIBBS	1866 - 1870
Charles EYNON	1870 - 1876
William John PORTER	1877 - 1886
Thomas Owen PROSSER	1886 - 1889
Henry Alban BROWN	1890 - 1906
George Henry LEA	1908 - 1911
George E JARVIS	1912 - 1931
Arthur Robert DOWN	1932 - 1933
Donald Sinclair SIMMONS	1933 - 1936
David John ROBERTS	1937 - 1937
George Henry CLOTHIER	1938 - 1943
John DAVIES (lay minister)	1944 - 1946
Alec George HUTCHINGS	1947 - 1975
A Barry BLAKE-LOBB	1977 - 1979
Eric G NEWMAN	1981 - 1988
Daryl E JONES	1990 - 1998
Martin MOORE	2000 - 2010
David J HORTON	2013 -

26678214R00120

Printed in Great Britain
by Amazon